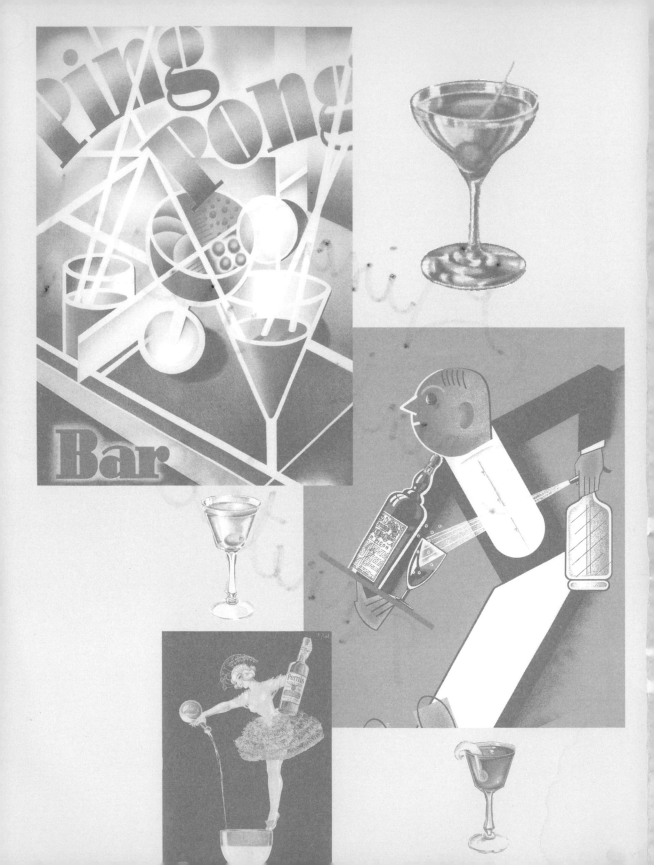

Make Mine

Vodka

Make Mine

Vodka

250 CLASSIC

COCKTAILS AND CUTTING-

EDGE INFUSIONS

SUSAN WAGGONER AND
ROBERT MARKEL

STEWART, TABORI & CHANG
NEW YORK

Editor: Dervla Kelly
Designer: Kay Schuckhart/Blond on Pond
Production Manager: Jane Searle

Library of Congress Cataloging-in-Publication Data

Waggoner, Susan.
    Make mine vodka : 250 classic cocktails and cutting-edge infusions / by Susan Waggoner and Robert Markel.
        p. cm.
    Includes index.
    ISBN-13: 978-1-58479-543-8
    ISBN-10: 1-58479-543-3
    1. Cocktails. 2. Vodka. I. Markel, Robert. II. Title.

TX951.W2595 2006
641.8'74--dc22
2006008867

Published in 2006 by Stewart, Tabori & Chang
An imprint of Harry N. Abrams, Inc.

The text of this book was composed in Adobe Garamond

Printed and bound in Singapore
10 9 8 7 6 5 4 3 2 1

HNA ▮▮▯▯▯
harry n. abrams, inc.
a subsidiary of La Martinière Groupe

115 West 18th Street
New York, NY 10011
www.hnabooks.com

Contents

Vodka, the Clear Miracle

Vodka shall be taxed at a rate of two kopecks per bucketful.

— Eighteenth century Russian law

At the dawn of the millennium, the world was abuzz about a miraculous new spirit, as icy and bracing as the snow-frosted plains of its native lands. The Russians, who claimed to have invented it, called it *voda*. The Poles, who also claimed it as their own, called it *woda*. In either language, the word meant "*water*," an indication of how essential to life the libation was considered.

The spirit, of course, was vodka. And the millennium wasn't the one we rolled out the carpet for a few years back. It was the one that began a thousand years ago.

Today, vodka is still new, still exciting, and still winning devotees. From small batches brewed by locals, we've gone to distillers capable of bottling tides of the stuff to, in the past decade, discovering anew the joys of small local batches. We've gone from flavoring the spirit with local herbs and seeds to flavoring it with herbs from every corner of the world. The spirit whose clarity fills your martini glass was being drunk on the steppes when Leif Ericsson sailed for the New World. It had been around a few hundred years when Ghengis Khan swept across Asia. When you hold a vodka cocktail

in your hand, you've got ahold of over a thousand years of human history.

We think that's something to celebrate.

So, in appreciation of this sublimely blithe spirit, we offer *Make Mine Vodka*, a tribute to the lure and the lore of vodka, tips for perfect parties and flawless mixology, as well as recipes for 250 drinks, from the classics of old to today's cutting-edge cocktails.

VODKA IN THE WORLD

Vodka, the spirit we keep on ice, was born in a cold climate. And it was born *because* of a cold climate. Alcoholic beverages were not merely a by-product of mankind's thrill-seeking nature. They came about for reasons that were also practical, as safe-to-drink alternatives to easily contaminated water. But in the colder reaches of northern Europe, the earliest forms of spirits—beer, mead, and wine—shared one of water's common disadvantages. At very cold temperatures, their relatively low alcohol content could not prevent them from freezing. This made storage and shipping almost im-

possible for much of the year, but it also became a tool for innovation. In addition to icy solids, this natural freezing produced an icy slush with a bracingly high alcohol content. Soon, people were purposely brewing and freezing low-alcohol beverages to produce a new, more potent drink. The first purposeful, documented production of vodka in Russia dates back to the end of the first millennium.

From the beginning, Russians prized their new beverage. It's said that in A.D. 988, when the Grand Prince of Kiev decided it was time for his people to abandon paganism in favor of a monotheistic religion, he was ambivalent as to which faith to embrace. If anything, he gave a slight edge to Islam, for he appreciated the Moslems' political and military prowess. However, the mullahs explained that alcohol was strictly proscribed, whereas the Christian priests said that alcohol was allowed to all. This apparently sealed the deal, and the Grand Prince commanded his subjects to embrace Christianity.

By 1174, the first distillery had been es-

You know, vodka is for Russians what therapy is for Americans.

— Six Feet Under

tablished in Russia. Poland claims to have distilled a similar spirit as early as the eighth century, but whether or not it was a true vodka or something more closely related to brandy remains controversial.

No matter where they were made, early vodkas were crude by modern standards, and so harsh-tasting that producers often added herbs and other flavorings to mask the taste. Nevertheless, vodka was popular enough to be described as the national drink of Russia by the 1300s. Two hundred years later, it was the undisputed national drink of Poland and Finland as well.

A significant breakthrough came in the mid-1400s, when pot distillation was introduced. This made large-scale production possible and resulted in a purer, more reliable product. By the early 1500s, vodka

had become one of Russia's best-known exports. Soon Poland and Sweden were also mass-producing vodka, making it a regional phenomenon.

In both Russia and Poland, the right to produce vodka was largely reserved for members of the aristocracy, and vodka production and sale contributed to the income of many country estates. This resulted in a fairly abundant supply of vodka, but also a far from consistent product. There were no standards guaranteeing proof or purity, and the quality varied wildly from estate to estate and even season to season. By 1860, there were over five thousand producers of vodka in Russia alone. When the tsar's regime fell and the Bolsheviks seized control of all private distilleries a half century later, thousands of aristocrats fled, taking their vodka recipes and expertise with them.

Many of the fleeing tsarists landed in Paris, where they set about inventing new lives or reviving their old ones. In the latter group was a former distiller who began making and selling vodka under the French version of his family name—Smirnoff. This was the first step toward making vodka not just a national or regional favorite but a global spirit. Today, vodka is made not just in Russia, Poland, and Scandinavia but also in England, Holland, Germany, France, Italy, the United States, Canada, the Caribbean, Brazil, New Zealand, Australia, Japan, and other countries.

VODKA IN AMERICA

It wasn't long until Paris-based Smirnoff met a fellow Russian exile and formed a partnership to open a distillery in America, manufacturing vodka as well as other spirits. Smirnoff wasn't the first distiller to try to interest Americans in vodka. Wolfschmidt distilleries had tried decades earlier and been met with universal disinterest.

For Smirnoff, the timing was even worse. Prohibition had just ended. During the long, dry years of its reign, Americans had developed a taste for gin, for the simple reason that gin was the easiest spirit to counterfeit. Already established as the clear spirit of choice, gin made it hard for vodka to gain a toehold. Moreover, the generally abysmal quality of bathtub gin had left Americans slightly queasy. The idea of drinking a clear spirit straight up, without mixer or embellishment, was less than appetizing—yet taking shots neat was the way vodka had always been

drunk, and it didn't occur to Smirnoff to market it any other way.

A breakthrough of sorts came when the production line ran out of corks stamped "Smirnoff's Vodka." Since it was impractical to hold the vodka until more corks could be made, the company decided to use corks marked "Smirnoff's Whiskey" and market the vodka as a new type of whiskey, one without flavor, odor, or color. The idea caught on with the public, and sales turned the corner.

Unfortunately, just as vodka was beginning to catch on, World War II broke out. Distillers converted their production lines to war work, and soon liquor was a rare commodity. Although rationing technically allowed Americans to purchase a fifth of liquor a month, ration coupons were worthless if there was no product to be had. Referred to by many as "the second Prohibition," World War II left the country thirsting for the Scotch, whiskey, and gin from the good old days. Vodka, which was still new and slightly exotic, was probably the least missed of spirits.

Vodka's big break came in the decades just after the war, as America was settling into its long Cold War with the Soviet Union. As early as 1930, Harry Craddock of London's Savoy Hotel had included a vodka drink called the Moscow Mule in his *Savoy Cocktail Book*, but it's unclear that the drink ever made it to America. In 1962, with the Cold War headed toward the Cuban missile crisis and Rudolf Nureyev making his American debut, a bartender at the Cock 'n Bull in Hollywood decided to play off the interest in all things Sovietski by reintroducing the Moscow Mule. It was an instant sensation, and soon became a favorite coast to coast. For many Americans, the drink was the first vodka cocktail they'd ever tasted.

An even bigger boost came from another artifact of postwar culture—British

secret agent James Bond. The first Bond movie, *Dr. No*, appeared in 1962, and others followed at the breathtaking pace of nearly one a year. Played to an ultrasuave max by Sean Connery, Agent 007 set the standard for Cold War chic, and when moviegoers saw Bond express a preference for vodka over gin or whiskey, they hurried to do the same. For perhaps the first time, vodka versions of gin drinks like the Martini and the Gimlet became more popular than the originals.

Vodka, like other spirits, suffered a decline in popularity during 1970s. Hard liquor was suddenly considered stodgy and dreadfully behind the times, supplanted by a new interest in wine. The cocktail party of old was replaced, almost overnight, by wine and cheese tastings, and wine bars replaced cocktail lounges by the hundreds. Eventually, the last rind of Brie was scraped clean and people stopped thinking of *Zinfandel*, *Riesling*, and *Beaujolais* as extremely exotic, hyperstylish words. All it took was for a few bold style-setters to walk into a *boite*, brush aside the wine list, and ask for a Martini (shaken not stirred), and the cocktail era was back in full force, with vodka leading the way.

Vodka Primer

Virtually unknown in America until after World War II, in less than fifty years vodka became the Western world's single most popular spirit. Gin, at one time the über-clear, was dethroned, so clearly number two that bartenders no longer reached for it automatically upon hearing the word *Martini*, but asked instead, "Gin or vodka?" And more times than not, the answer was vodka. By the time the new millennium arrived, more than three hundred vodkas were on the market, and Americans were downing more than 480 million bottles of the stuff a year. Hardly a week passed without word of an exotic new infusion or new "signature" Martini being served up somewhere in town.

Despite all this, vodka has remained the most misunderstood of beverages. The person who will rave about a new micro-batch variety at fifty or a hundred dollars a bottle cannot, in all likelihood, tell you how this differs from mass-produced vodkas that cost substantially less, nor can most people tell you, correctly, how vodka differs from bourbon or tequila. And, while it doesn't take much knowledge to enjoy a good vodka cocktail, fully *appreciating* vodka takes knowledge.

5 VODKA MYTHS

**MYTH 1: VODKA IS MADE FROM POTA-
TOES.** Ask most people what vodka is
made from and they'll insist it's potatoes.
In fact, vodka can be made from any vegetable matter that can be fermented into a
mash rich in simple sugars. Although a few
potato-based vodkas are sold today, the
overwhelming majority are made from
wheat or other grains.

MYTH 2: VODKA IS ALWAYS CLEAR. We
can't blame you for this one. More than
likely, all the vodka you've ever seen has
been clear. But that doesn't
mean it has to be. Whether or
not vodka is clear or brown
largely depends on whether
it was made in a column
still (the most common variety for this spirit) or a
pot still (as used for
scotch and cognac).
Column stills are pre-
ferred as more efficient
for vodka production,

and people now expect the look and taste
of column-distilled vodka. But in parts of
eastern Europe, you may still come across
brown-hued pot-distilled brands.

**MYTH 3: VODKA WILL NOT GIVE YOU A
HANGOVER.** The mark of a good vodka is
its purity and absence of flavor—qualities
that are achieved by multiple filtrations.
The purer the result, the fewer hangover-
causing elements the vodka contains.
However, vodka is still an alcoholic spirit,
and drinking to excess certainly can—and
will—cause a hangover.

**MYTH 4: ALL VODKA IS FLAVORLESS
AND TASTES THE SAME.** By custom (and
law, if you're an American distiller), vodka is
a neutral spirit, without an identifiable
scent, taste, or color. This does not, however, mean that all vodkas taste the same.
Read the results of any taste test and you'll
see what we mean. Invariably, phrases like
"lemony," "hint of vanilla," or "slightly pep-
pery" appear. This is partly because, hard as
distillers may try, there is no way to rob

vodka of 100 percent of its base flavors. And because, at the fine end of the spectrum, qualities like smoothness and finish become almost indistinguishable from taste.

MYTH 5: THE MORE EXPENSIVE THE BOTTLE, THE BETTER THE VODKA.

Well, perhaps. While it's true that bargain-basement vodkas will have been cheaply made, without the multiple filtrations required to eliminate harshness, it's just as true that spending a lot may buy you nothing but bragging rights. A now-famous taste test conducted by the *New York Times* pitted twenty-one vodkas, ranging from humble house favorites to micro batches costing three times as much, against each other. To the consternation of many experts, the all-around favorite by a wide margin was the "ordinary" vodka that's been around for years—Smirnoff. The *Times* concluded that, "Unlike most other spirits and certainly unlike beer and wine, vodka does not necessarily benefit from artisanal manufacturing."[1]

---

1. Asimov, Eric: "A Humble Old Label Ices Its Rivals" *New York Times*, January 26, 2005.

WHAT IS VODKA MADE OF?

As we said above, vodka can be made of almost any vegetable matter than can be converted into a sugar-rich mash. Early vodkas were made from the most abundant, least-expensive crop—potatoes. And, while there are some fine potato-based vodkas made today, most manufacturers prefer grain-based mashes, either all wheat, all rye, or a combination of grains. But wheat is by no means the only base for modern vodkas. Vodka is also made with corn, barley, grapes, and even sugar cane.

No matter what base is used, it isn't vodka's main ingredient. The main ingredient in any vodka is . . . (drum roll, please) . . . water. That's right, *water*. And the water *does* make a difference. Different waters have very different qualities—flat or tangy, pure, acidic, metallic, and so on. This is why distillers often advertise that their vodka is made from spring water, from melted snow, or from a previously untapped aquifer. One company even uses water from twelve-thousand-year-old icebergs, claiming them as the purest of all sources.

HOW VODKA IS MADE

Making vodka is relatively simple, as no aging is required. First the grain, potatoes, or other base ingredients are fermented. The wash produced by fermentation is then distilled into a high-proof spirit. At this stage, a high-alcohol "vodka" exists, but it is still in such a raw, primitive stage that most people would find it undrinkable. This is why good vodkas undergo multiple distillations, with each pass creating a product that is smoother and higher in alcohol content. However, even repeated distillations cannot make an acceptably pure vodka, so the next step is lengthy filtration, usually through charcoal. The resulting product is clear and pure. It is also lethally high in alcohol—as high as 190 proof, or 95 percent alcohol, so water is added to dilute the vodka to 80 proof (40 percent alcohol). If the vodka is to be a flavored variety, this is the point at which the flavoring is added, and the spirit is ready for bottling.

Of course, this only sounds simple. Infinite choices made along the way—such as the recipe of the mash, the size and shape of the distilling vat, the material the vat is made of—and how well each step is carried out determine whether the end result is a truly superior vodka or one that is not worth drinking.

HOW TO TASTE VODKA

One of the real joys of vodka is learning how to taste it properly and use your experiences to guide your buying choices. We're not talking about becoming the equivalent of a wine snob. As we pointed out earlier, expense doesn't have a lot to do with what people find preferable in a good vodka. In fact, we encourage you to learn to taste vodka so you can *avoid* becoming a snob. Knowing what you're tasting and being confident about it will keep you from becoming the kind of person who believes that any vodka that costs more is necessarily better. Here are some pointers that will make you a tasting expert.

* **KEEP A NOTEBOOK.** Record your taste experiences in a notebook. Note the brand and type of the vodka, or paste in the label, and note the cost. Record your impressions of characteristics (described below) such as aroma, taste, mouth feel, and finish. Most of all, note your overall personal assessment. Do you feel that this vodka is worth its price? Is it one that stands up on its own, sipped straight, or is it an adequate but not spectacular vodka that would work best in cocktails? Are its quality and price so high that mixing it would be a travesty? What are its strengths? Where do its weaknesses lie? Most of all, did you enjoy the vodka enough to buy it again, or would you rather try something different next time?

* **CHOOSE AND PREPARE THE VODKA.** The best way to taste vodka is to have another vodka to compare it to. Choose a group of three to five vodkas for your tasting group, and put them in the freezer the night before your tasting. Freezing vodka makes the flavors vibrant and easy to evaluate. If the vodka is too warm, flavors tend to become muddled and drab.

✳ **CHOOSE YOUR GLASSES.** Only use glass glasses—no plastic, please! Shot glasses or cordial glasses with a two- to three-ounce capacity work best. At least an hour before your tasting, place glasses in the freezer so they can develop a good chill.

✳ **TAKE YOUR TIME.** Don't decide to have an impromptu tasting session when you have only a few minutes to spare. Pick a time when you can relax, and plan to spend five to ten minutes on each sample. This may sound excessive, but that's really the amount of time needed to take note of the full range of a spirit's characteristics.

✳ **POUR A HEALTHY SHOT.** You're going to need more than just a taste of vodka. Pour at least a generous ounce into your glass.

✳ **DEFROST.** Hold the glass a moment to take the frozen edge off. While you don't want the vodka too warm, you don't want to freeze your taste buds to a state of numbness, either.

✳ **SWIRL.** While you're holding your glass, swirl it gently. Notice the drops that cling to the side of the glass. These drops, known as "tears" or "legs," tell you something about the vodka in the glass. Long drops indicate a high-alcohol vodka that is likely to have a pleasing texture.

* **SMELL.** Swirling the vodka also helps release the vodka's aroma. Holding the glass about an inch from your nose, *gently* inhale—inhaling too deeply or too long will numb your nose. Make note of the first thing the scent reminds you of, even if it seems far-fetched. If you taste vodkas made from different substances, you'll discover that the base ingredient greatly influences the aroma. Grain-based vodkas, for example, actually smell faintly like bread, while potato-based vodkas smell earthier.

* **TAKE THE FIRST TASTE.** Take a sip. Let the vodka roll over your tongue and hold the vodka in your mouth as you exhale through your nose—you will get a second layer of scents. Note the vodka's taste and texture. Does it have a round, slightly oily mouth feel? A pleasant sting? A sensation of dryness?

* **TAKE A SECOND TASTE.** Now take a sip and swallow it immediately. This will tell you about the vodka's finish. Does it go down smoothly or is there a harsh burn?

Do the flavor and the essence of the vodka linger in your mouth or vanish as soon as you swallow? How does the experience of swallowing the vodka straight compare to swallowing the vodka after you held it in your mouth?

* **JOT DOWN YOUR IMPRESSIONS.** Record your observations now, before cleansing your palate or moving on to the next vodka.

* **CLEANSE YOUR PALATE.** Not everyone believes that cleansing the palate between vodkas is necessary. We recommend it, however. Just make sure not to cleanse your palate with anything that will leave traces of taste or aroma. Tepid water or unsalted crackers are ideal.

THROW A VODKA PARTY

So much vodka, so little time. A good way to gain a lot of knowledge in a little time is to throw a vodka party. That way, you and your friends can mix, taste, evaluate, share impressions, and have fun doing it.

A **Vodka Tasting Party** is a great way to try different flavors or brands, as well as a great way to sample a broad range of homemade infusions. Putting each invitee in charge of making an infusion to bring also cuts down the amount of work you have to do, and gives everyone a chance to be creative. Stock up on shot glasses, and give each guest his or her own notebook to record impressions. Compare findings to see which vodkas were the clear winners and why, and take note of which vodkas you definitely want to try again.

If your repertoire of mixed drinks needs some livening up, consider a **Martini Lounge Party**. Stock up on vodka and vermouth, add some flavored vodkas and liqueurs, and lay out a smorgasbord of exciting additives and garnishes, including fresh basil, rosemary, and other herbs; bite-sized fruits and vegetables; brined treats like capers, exotic olives, and pickled peppers; even a selection of sweets such as sugared berries, chocolate, candied citrus peel, and crystallized ginger. Type up some of the Martini recipes from this book and post

them beside the appropriate ingredients. Then let your guests run wild—and don't be surprised if they get inspired and come up with something new and delicious.

Tip: A fifth of vodka will yield about 16 cocktails or 25 (1-ounce) tastes.

PARTY À LA RUSSE

The liquor may be the same, but the traditions surrounding vodka drinking in Russia are as different from American customs as east is from west. And while you may prefer the ways you're already familiar with, a true connoisseur will take time to learn—and occasionally practice—the Russian style. After all, you never know when you'll find yourself in St. Petersburg with a long night to kill and new friends to be made.

If you really want to fit in, your first step is to be humble. Realize that almost everything you think you know about drinking vodka—all the cocktail recipes and garnishes, your preference for one mixer over another, your disdain for adulterating the vodka experience with food, and your pride in fancy glasses—is wrong in the eyes of

Russian and Polish vodka drinkers. To them, you are just another Westerner who doesn't really know how to drink. All these little flourishes distract from the vodka itself, and seem designed get the drinker quickly and inexpensively drunk rather than allowing him to stay sober (or almost sober) for as many rounds as possible. Indeed, if you go to an authentic vodka-drinking party, you will see a businesslike table set up with the essentials and little more—bottles of vodka, the plainest of glasses, and food selected not for its taste but for chemical properties that prolong the drinker's staying power.

Here are some basics to help you go with the flow.

✳ **VODKA, ALL VODKA, AND NOTHING BUT VODKA.** A party worthy of a tsar will serve only one beverage—vodka. No beer, wine, soda, or other alternatives.

✳ **DRINK IT NEAT.** Traditionally, vodka is drunk straight, without mixers or garnishes.

✳ **DRINK IT ALL.** Drinkers are expected to down the contents of the glass in one go. Sipping shows a lack of enthusiasm for wholeheartedly joining in with one's companions. (Choose the smallest glass you can find, and don't let your host fill it too full.)

✳ **DRINK WITH THE CROWD.** In Russia, everyone drinks together. Literally. At a serious vodka party, someone offers a toast, and glasses are emptied in one communal gulp. Then no one drinks again until the next toast is offered. Dominating a bottle,

pouring and drinking on your own, is considered rude or, at best, lacking in social grace.

✳ **OFFER A TOAST.** Everyone at the party is expected to make a toast. Typically, the person about to offer the toast first goes from person to person, pouring vodka and making sure all glasses are filled. Be prepared to jump in and do your part.

✳ **STAND A ROUND.** If the party is in a bar or restaurant, everyone at the party should buy a round for everyone else once during the course of the evening.

✳ **HAVE A BITE.** Between rounds, Russians eat *zakuski*, special foods whose composition buffers the effects of the alcohol. Most *zakuski* are acidic, salty, or oily. Slices of lemon, pickles, marinated tomatoes, salted cucumbers, caviar, as well as herrings, sardines, or other fish in oil are all typical items served, often accompanied by cold boiled potatoes or blini. Small sips of mineral water may be taken to clear the palate.

* **PACE YOURSELF.** Keeping pace with the crowd for the first three rounds is enough to establish your sociability and friendliness. After that, you can sit out rounds, joining in only occasionally. Unless you were brought up on the steppes, it's unlikely you will ever keep pace with the number of toasts given and glasses poured.

* **MIND THE EMPTIES.** Empty bottles should be placed on the floor beside a table leg, and never returned to the table. This is because empty bottles suggest poverty and want, exactly the opposite impression the party is trying to create.

* **GO THE DURATION IF YOU CAN.** To Russians, the idea of a cocktail party of two or three hours is a mystery. Serious vodka drinking can go on for hours and hours and hours. *Zakuski* may be followed by hot dishes and a sit-down dinner, where everyone is expected to contribute to the flow of lively and energetic conversation. More vodka is drunk, and the party finally ends with assorted cakes and glasses of steaming hot tea.

TIP: We're told that Russians who are serious about their drinking fortify themselves before parties by eating a few cold potatoes, downing some raw eggs, and topping it off with a few spoonfuls of olive oil—a menu that would make us take to our bed long before the party began.

FOOD FOR YOUR VODKA

Food is a party must—especially when alcohol is being consumed. Traditional accompaniments include caviar and blini, boiled eggs, and boiled potatoes—items that may be too expensive, too difficult to make, or too plain to be a hit. However, you can echo the tastes of these items with a few clever substitutions—affordable taramasalata, for example, instead of hundred-

Come for Cocktails

dollar-an-ounce beluga, or deviled eggs instead of plain hard-boiled ones. Here's our list of vodka-compatible snacks.

Dips, Spreads, and Finger Foods

Assorted cheeses: sharp, noncreamy cheeses such as cheddar, gorgonzola, blue, Swiss, and pepper Jack

Assorted fruits: melon wedges or balls, fresh pineapple and berries, apple and pear slices, and mango cubes

Assorted meats: robust deli meats such as ham, thinly sliced roast beef, pickle loaf, and smoked turkey

Bagna cauda

Bruschetta

Buffalo chicken wings

Caviar dip or spread

Ceviche

Cheese spreads that are strong and flavorful, such as blue cheese, wine cheddar, and horseradish

Cherry tomatoes soaked in plain, black pepper, or chili vodka

Cornichons

Deviled eggs

Guacamole

Herring, either pickled or in sauce

Hummus

Marinated vegetables

New potato halves garnished with sour cream and caviar

Nuts, roasted and salted

Olives

Onion dip

Pickled beets

Pickled onions

Radishes

Salsa

Scallions

Smoked salmon spread

Steak tartare

Stuffed mushrooms

Tapenade

Taramasalata

Platforms and Dippers

Bagel chips

Breadsticks

Crackers

Crostini

Party rye

Pita triangles

Rye crisps

Toast points

Tortilla chips

Here's How

It's amazing how many people only *think* they know how to mix a good cocktail. The best ingredients and recipes go only so far. If a drink is haphazardly mixed and shoddily served, it will never taste the way it's supposed to, and never garner the sighs of delight from its drinkers. If it's been a while since you mixed a great cocktail, it's time to brush up.

FIVE STEPS TO PERFECT MIXING

✳ **USE CLEAN, DRY EQUIPMENT.** Shakers, shot glasses, and other utensils should be washed and dried between drinks to eliminate traces of previous cocktails. If you're mixing for a crowd, it's a good idea to have a double set of everything.

✳ **START COLD, FINISH COLDER.** Cold is always an essential in a good cocktail, but even more so in a vodka cocktail. Store your vodka in the refrigerator or, if you can, the freezer. Use only juices and mixers that have been thoroughly chilled, and have plenty of ice on hand. If your cocktail is to be strained into a glass without ice, take time to chill your glasses ahead of time.

A GOOD MIXER

THE SHAKE 'EM UP GIRL

✱ **MEASURE AND MIX CAREFULLY.** Because cocktails contain a relatively small amount of each ingredient, the margin for error is narrow and eyeballing is never a good idea. Nor is it a good idea to *stir* when the directions say *shake*, or similarly improvise. A haphazardly mixed drink is an unknown quantity. Take the time to do it right and you will be rewarded with a great-tasting drink every time.

✱ **KNOW THE TECHNIQUES.** There's a right way to do everything—even things you think you already know. If you think "shake" means a few up and down tosses or aren't quite sure what "muddle" means, take a few minutes to review the terminology, which is explained on page 27.

✱ **PRESENTATION.** Looks count, so take time to make sure your cocktail is well turned out. For an imaginative touch, see our list of **Great Garnishes** on page 38. Make sure that whatever garnish you use, even if it is only a simple slice of orange or lemon, is fresh, cleanly cut, and appealing. Wipe spills and droplets from the cocktail glass and always present your creation on a crisp, clean napkin.

HELPFUL MEASUREMENTS & CONVERSIONS

1 gill = 5 oz.

1 jigger or shot = 1½ oz.

1 pony = 1 oz.

1 dash = 4 to 5 drops

3 tsp. = 1 tbsp.

1 tbsp. = ½ oz.

4 tbsp. = ¼ c.

1 c. = 8 oz.

Juice of ½ fresh lime = approx. ½ oz.

Juice of ½ fresh lemon = approx. ½ to ¾ oz. depending on size

2 sugar cubes = ½ tsp. sugar

METRIC EQUIVALENTS

1 fifth (25.6 oz.) = 750ml

1 pint = 472ml

1 c. = 236ml

1½ oz. = 44.355ml

1 oz. = 29.57ml

1 tbsp. = 15ml

1 tsp. = 5ml

TERMS AND TECHNIQUES

❋ **CRACKED ICE.** Cracked ice is ideal for shaking cocktails to icy perfection because it offers more surface area than ice cubes but will not melt as quickly as crushed ice. An efficient method of cracking ice is to fill a heavy-duty resealable freezer bag halfway with ice, cover with a towel, and hit with a hammer.

❋ **FLOAT.** The purpose of floating cream, liqueur, or some other liquid atop a drink is to add taste and color without mixing it into the drink. Therefore, avoid pouring the float ingredient directly into the cocktail. Instead, pour it over the back of a spoon, or tilt the glass and gently pour it against the side of the glass. You can also pour the liquid into a spoon, lower, and slide it gently atop the cocktail.

❋ **JUICE.** To get the most juice from a lemon or lime, make sure the fruit is at room temperature. Roll the fruit under your hand on a counter or table top to help tissues release their juices, then cut and squeeze, being sure to strain out the seeds. If you forgot to remove your fruit from the refrigerator in time, 20 to 40 seconds in a microwave should do the trick; just let it cool before cutting. You can also increase the juice yield by soaking the fruit in warm water for several minutes.

MUDDLE. Muddling is done to break down tissues of fruits or herbs to facilitate the release and mingling of flavors. Place ingredients in the glass or shaker as instructed, and press or twist with a muddler or similar blunt, heavy utensil, such as a pestle.

RIM A GLASS. Rimming the edge of a glass, usually with sugar or salt, is done to add taste as well as a decorative touch. The trick is to keep the substance on the *outside* rim of the glass. If the inside is rimmed as well, the substance will gradually dissolve into the drink and change its flavor. To make sure this doesn't happen, carefully rub the adhering agent (such as a citrus wedge or liqueur) only on the outside edge of the glass. Then pour the sugar or salt onto a small plate and, holding the glass at a slight angle, roll the moistened outer rim to pick up granules. Let the glass dry for a few minutes before filling it.

SHAKE. It's sad to see people give their cocktails only a few half-hearted shakes before pouring them into glasses. The purpose of *shaking* a cocktail isn't just to give ingredients a nodding acquaintance with each other—it's to thoroughly combine them and make them as cold as the ice they're tumbling over. You can't do this in three or four seconds. When we say shake, we mean *shake* vigorously, in an even rhythm, for a good 15 seconds—until the shaker is almost too cold to handle.

TWIST. Was there ever a more misunderstood term in all of drink making? A twist is a narrow strip of citrus peel, about 1½" long and ¼" wide, scraped of excess pith. To garnish with a twist means to hold the twist horizontally an inch or so above the drink, peel side down, and twist the ends in opposite directions so that a few drops of essence fall into the drink and float on the surface. It's customary to then drop the twist into the drink. Sadly, we've observed many an uninformed imbiber fish the twist from the drink and repeat the whole process—unnecessarily.

ZEST. Zest (from a citrus fruit) is much finer than a twist and has little or no pith attached to the bright surface peel. Zest may be gathered with a fine grater or with a zester, which produces longer, threadlike pieces.

BASIC BAR GEAR

You don't need to have an elaborate bar to mix great drinks, nor do you need to invest in a lot of expensive equipment. With a few exceptions, a lot of what you need can be borrowed from your own kitchen. In fact, the only pieces of equipment you really should invest in are a good cocktail shaker with a strainer and a marked shot glass or jigger for measuring. Shot glasses are very inexpensive, and can be purchased almost anywhere these days, including the grocery store. Shakers are another matter, and can range from a few dollars to a few hundred. Fortunately, there's not much relationship between the quality of the shaker and its price. You can get a great shaker for a modest amount of money, or spend a great deal of money on an item that's more conversation piece than reliable tool. Our only recommendation is to look

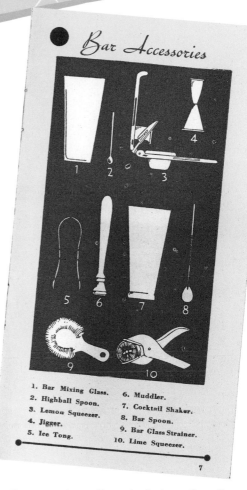

Bar Accessories

1. Bar Mixing Glass.
2. Highball Spoon.
3. Lemon Squeezer.
4. Jigger.
5. Ice Tong.
6. Muddler.
7. Cocktail Shaker.
8. Bar Spoon.
9. Bar Glass Strainer.
10. Lime Squeezer.

for a simple, well-made shaker of medium-weight metal, ideally fitted with a strainer.

Here's our complete list of items for a home bar, but please don't rush out and buy everything at once. Part of the fun is acquiring items as you go along.

Cutting board

Paring knife

Zester or vegetable peeler

Reamer, squeezer, or juicer

Muddler

Blender or ice crusher

Bar towels

Toothpicks or garnish picks

Swizzle sticks

Cocktail napkins

GLASSES

Of course, you will need something to serve your cocktails in. Some people go crazy acquiring multiple sets of glasses—martini glasses, double martini glasses, champagne flutes and champagne coups, tiki mugs and hurricane glasses and snifters and cordial glasses and on and on. Well, if you have the storage space and the money and the desire for all that, fine. But you can get by very well with just a few basic types:

COCKTAIL GLASS. A stemmed glass with a classic, funnel-shaped cup, the standard

Cocktail shaker

Strainer

Ice bucket and tongs

Marked shot glass or jigger

Measuring spoons

Liquid measuring cup

Bar spoon or long-handled spoon, such as an iced tea spoon

barware for Martinis or any cocktail served without ice. Although showy, large-capacity versions (holding from 6 oz. on up) are attention getting, our advice is to go for smaller, conventional-capacity glasses at home. There's no point in making a large "double" cocktail that will separate and become warm before you can drink it.

COLLINS GLASS. A tall glass with a small diameter, often frosted, intended for drinks made with a relatively large amount of mixer and served with lots of ice.

HIGHBALL GLASS. Shorter than a collins glass and with a slightly larger diameter, meant to hold ice, a single spirit, and 3 to 4 oz. of mixer.

OLD FASHIONED GLASS. Also known as a "rocks" (or "on the rocks") glass. A short, wide-diameter glass made to hold ice and straight spirits or a cocktail with just a few ounces of added ingredients. If you don't have highball glasses, old fashioned glasses will do.

SHOT GLASS. Since vodka is often enjoyed straight up, these small glasses, holding no more than 2 oz., come in quite handy.

THANK YOU, MR. SINDLER!

The swizzle stick we consider so essential today wasn't invented until Prohibition had come and gone. Sitting with a friend in the bar of the Ritz Carlton in Boston, enjoying one of the first legal Martinis he'd had since the Great Experiment ended, Jay Sindler noted that there was no elegant way to remove his olive from the glass. Sindler, an engineer and inventor, lost no time in creating and patenting a handy little item he called a swizzle stick. Within three years, Sindler had quit his day job to produce swizzle sticks full time. Swizzle sticks were soon followed by cocktail picks and swords, coffee stirrers, steak markers, menu clips, coasters, napkins, and eventually hanging pink plastic elephants and brightly colored monkeys, mermaids, camels, and giraffes.

STOCKING A VODKA BAR

As with equipment, you don't need to spend a lot of money to stock a bar with a few minimal basics. Except for the vodka itself, most basics are inexpensive grocery-store items, and since not all ingredients are needed for every drink, which items become "musts" for you depends very much on your personal preferences.

VODKA. You could easily fill an entire bar with nothing but vodka—plain vodka and premium, grain-based and grape-based and exotic microbrews, and dozens of flavors. Please don't. Take some time to explore this spirit and determine your personal tastes first. Start with a good but nonpremium plain vodka for cocktails and one or two basic flavors that appeal to you. We heartily endorse experimenting with your own infusions (recipes can be found starting on page 125), so you may want to make the plain bottle a large size for economy's sake. If you enjoy your vodka straight, you may also want to buy a slightly more expensive variety as well.

LIQUEURS. Liqueurs are a perfect match with vodka—just think of the famous Black Russian! By far the most common liqueur used in vodka cocktails is orange, such as triple sec or cointreau, so it's a good basic to have on hand. Coffee and other fruit-flavored liqueurs, especially berry, are also popular with vodka.

JUICES. Orange, tomato, and cranberry juices are classic foundations for numerous vodka cocktails, but don't limit yourself to the known suspects. Try exotics like mango, pomegranate, and guava. To maximize money and refrigerator space, buy single-serve sizes, and always have juices well chilled before mixing your cocktails.

MIXERS. Like juices, carbonated mixers should be well chilled before mixing begins—cold is such an important factor in a good vodka cocktail that mixers starting from room temperature will just never attain the coldness they really should have. The most common mixer for vodka is a well-balanced lemon-lime soda.

GRENADINE AND OTHER SYRUPS. Syrups are a great way to add flavor and color to your drinks. Grenadine, available in any grocery store, is still the most commonly used syrup, but recent years have seen a proliferation of exotic syrups, including berry, coffee, caramel, maraschino, tropical fruit flavors, and various nut fla-

vors, including an old classic, almond-flavored orgeat. If you want to experiment with a variety of flavors, syrups can be a less expensive alternative to liqueurs.

ROSE'S LIME JUICE. Though not a syrup, Rose's lime *is* sweetened. It's a staple in numerous drinks, including a Gimlet, and can be used in a pinch when you've run out of fresh limes.

CITRUS FRUITS. Look for fruits that are fully mature and have a weighty feel, as immature fruits seldom reach their full level of juiciness. Since most of the cocktails you make will call for a slice, wedge, or twist of citrus, choose fruits with smooth, unblemished, unwrinkled skin. Once home, store fruits in the refrigerator—exposure to light can discolor skin, and room temperature speeds decay.

BITTERS. Bitters are highly potent distillations of alcohol and spices, added to cocktails by the drop to add a dash of counterpoint. The most common of these,

Angostura, is so well known that when recipes say simply "bitters," they invariably mean Angostura. Also well known is Peychaud's bitters, a lighter, slightly sweeter concoction than Angostura. Orange bitters are also popular, and no longer as difficult to find as they were just a decade ago.

SUGAR. In addition to the sugar you will need to make your own infusions and syrups, you will want to keep a small amount of sugar handy for rimming glasses and, occasionally, sweetening cocktails.

SALT. Use coarse, large-crystal salt for rimming glasses, but don't spend a fortune on exotic varieties—you can buy an inexpensive box of kosher salt in almost any grocery store.

WORCESTERSHIRE AND PEPPER SAUCES. A must if you're going to try your hand at Bloody Marys.

Basics You Can Make At Home

SIMPLE SYRUP. Combine equal parts sugar and water in a heavy saucepan. Bring to a boil, stirring constantly to dissolve the sugar. Reduce the heat and gently simmer until the mixture becomes a clear syrup, about 5 minutes. Remove from the heat, cool, and store in a clean, tightly covered jar in the refrigerator. One cup of water and 1 cup of sugar will yield approximately 1½ cups simple syrup.

SWEET AND SOUR MIX. Combine equal parts water, sugar, lemon juice, and lime juice. Stir until the sugar is completely dissolved and store in a lidded bottle or jar in the refrigerator.

GINGER SYRUP. Coarsely chop fresh ginger, with peel on, to make 1 cup (about 4 oz.). Transfer to a heavy saucepan and add 1 cup water and ½ cup sugar. Bring to a boil, then reduce the heat and simmer gently for 15 minutes. Strain the mixture, cool, and transfer to a lidded jar or bottle. Store in the refrigerator.

CANDIED ORANGE OR LEMON PEEL. Use a vegetable peeler or the channel knife of a zester to cut long, thin strips of peel, taking as little of the white pith as possible. In a large, heavy saucepan or pot, combine equal parts sugar and water, making sure you will have enough to more than cover the peel when you add it. Bring the syrup to a boil, stirring to dissolve the sugar. Lower the heat and boil gently for 5 minutes, stirring occasionally. Add the peel, lower the heat, and simmer gently for 15 minutes. Remove with a slotted spoon and transfer to a baking sheet to dry. When the strips are nearly dry but still flexible, wrap them around a wooden spoon handle, thin dowel, or pencil, then let them finish drying completely—you will have attractive spirals that can be snipped into shorter lengths and hooked over the rim of a glass for an attractive garnish. Don't throw away the syrup—it makes a delicious cocktail additive. Store candied peel in a tightly lidded plastic container.

CANDIED LIME PEEL. Cut long, thin

Without olives, a Martini just doesn't quite make it.

Elliot Gould mixes a Martini in *M*A*S*H*, 1970

strips of peel as described above. Place in a saucepan and cover with cold water. Bring to a boil. Drain. Repeat this two more times, then proceed as for candied orange or lemon peel above, making a simple syrup, boiling for 5 minutes, then adding the peel and simmering for 15 minutes. After the peel is transferred to a baking sheet to dry, sprinkle generously with more sugar, then let dry completely. Store in a tightly lidded plastic container.

CHERRY BOMBS. Cherry bombs are made from that classic staple, the maraschino cherry. To prepare, drain all but about 10 percent of the liquid from a jar of cherries, then refill with a spirit or liqueur of your choosing, such as vodka or flavored vodka, brandy, or orange liqueur, and macerate at least overnight. If you want further embellishment, dip cherries in melted white or dark chocolate, let set, then use for garnish.

GREAT GARNISHES

Because it's the perfect canvas, vodka has spawned dozens of cocktails that are almost more appetizer than cocktail, with flavor themes and taste bursts that enliven the palate. When it comes to garnishes, these cocktails cry out for a creative touch, and now's the time for you to add an imaginative signature all your own. Some master mixologists tie thin strips of citrus peel into tiny knots, others use aspic cutters or small cookie cutters to cut pieces of fruit into stars, moons, and tiny hearts. Still others buy their olives unstuffed so they can stuff them with everything from lemon peel to hazelnuts to blue cheese to tiny chili peppers. There are really no givens anymore, and coming up with innovative garnishes for your cocktails is part of the fun. Here are fifty ideas to start you thinking:

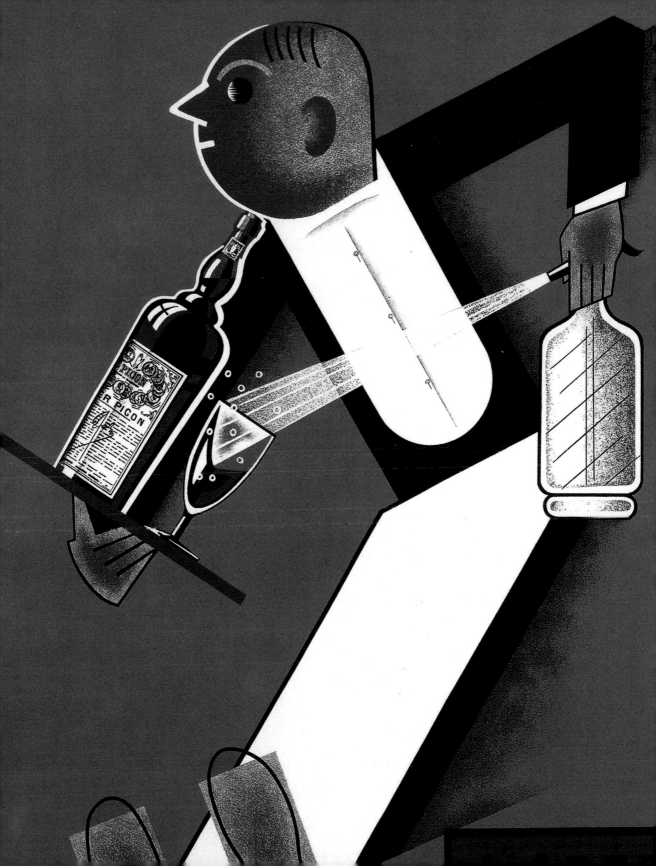

Apple slice
Basil, fresh
Blackberries
Blueberries
Candied citrus peel
Candied ginger slice
Capers
Cherry bomb (see page 36)
Cherry or grape tomato
Cinnamon stick
Cranberries, canned or frozen, drained
Cucumber slice
Dill, fresh

Edible flowers (only use blossoms that have been grown, pesticide free, for consumption)
Edible gold dust (available from cake or candy supply stores)
Espresso beans
Grapes, frozen
Kiwi slice
Kumquat slice
Lemon twist, wedge, or slice
Lemongrass stalk, fresh or dried
Lime twist, wedge, or slice
Lychee, canned
Mango cubes or slices
Maraschino cherry
Melon balls
Mint, fresh
Nuts, lightly toasted
Olives, black or green
Orange or blood orange twist, wedge, or slice
Oregano, fresh

Pear slice
Pineapple cubes
Pickled beet slice
Pickled green tomato, these days known as a "tomolive"
Pickled mushroom
Pickled pearl onion
Pickled spiced green beans, okra, or other baby vegetable
Radish slice
Raspberries
Rosemary, fresh
Scallion
Star anise
Starfruit, sliced
Strawberries
Sun-dried tomato slice
Tangerine or clementine section
Tarragon, fresh
Thyme, fresh
Tomato chip (thinly slice fresh tomatoes, arrange on baking sheet, and dry in a warm oven)

Alexander the Great

Purportedly invented by crooner Nelson Eddy, and a clear forerunner of the ever-popular White Russian.

1 ½ oz. vodka
½ oz. crème de cacao
½ oz. coffee liqueur
½ oz. cream

Pour ingredients into a cocktail shaker filled with ice. Shake vigorously, then strain into a chilled cocktail glass.

Anno 1960

This drink debuted the same year as another Italian classic, Fellini's *La Dolce Vita*. We like to drink it and think of Anita Ekberg wading in the Trevi Fountain.

1 ½ oz. vodka
¾ oz. dry vermouth
¾ oz. Campari

Pour ingredients into a cocktail shaker filled with ice. Shake briskly, then strain into a chilled cocktail glass. Garnish with a thin twist of lemon.

Appletini

By all accounts, the Appletini originated at Lola's in West Hollywood in the 1990s. It became an instant classic, and soon almost everyone had his own favorite recipe. Here, for those who may never have had it, is the original.

2 oz. vodka
1 oz. apple schnapps
Splash of sweet and sour mix

Pour ingredients into a cocktail shaker filled with ice. Shake, then strain into a chilled cocktail glass. Garnish with a thin, freshly cut slice of apple.

FOR YOUR FURTHER DRINKING PLEASURE: There are almost endless variations of this drink and, frankly, we love them all. Here are a few of our favorites, all shaken with ice, strained into a chilled cocktail glass, and garnished with apple.

ALOHA APPLETINI: 1 ½ oz. vodka, 1 oz. apple schnapps, ¾ oz. pineapple juice, and a splash of lemon-lime soda.

CARAMEL APPLETINI: 1 ½ oz. vodka, ¾ oz. apple schnapps and ¾ oz. butterscotch schnapps

CINNAMON APPLETINI: 1 oz. vodka, ½ oz. cinnamon vodka, ¾ oz. calvados, 1 oz. apple juice or cider.

GREEN APPLETINI: 2 oz. vodka, 1 oz. apple schnapps, splash of melon liqueur.

SOUR APPLETINI: 2 oz. vodka, 1 oz. apple schnapps, splash of sweet and sour mix, and the juice of ½ lime.

Balalaika

Like the triangle-shaped, three-stringed Russian folk instrument for which it was named, this drink builds complexity from just three ingredients.

1 oz. vodka
1 oz. orange liqueur
Juice of 1 lemon

Pour ingredients into a cocktail shaker filled with ice. Shake briskly, then strain into a chilled cocktail glass.

FOR YOUR FURTHER DRINKING PLEASURE: A lovely variation on the Balalaika's strings is the **Blue Balalaika**, made by adding 1 oz. blue curaçao to the recipe above and garnishing with a twist of lemon.

NAME GAMES

Westerners these days have adopted vodka as thoroughly their own, but once upon a time it was as distant and mysterious as the steppes of Siberia itself. To sip a vodka cocktail was to sip something exotic, intensely foreign, and all but unknown. Mixologists capitalized on this, and a good way to spot a vintage era vodka cocktail is by its name. If it summons images of tsars and tsarinas, dancing peasants and Fabergé eggs, it's probably a drink that dates backs to the 1920s or '30s, as is the case with the revered Balalaika, the Czarina, the Tovarich, and the ethereal Ballet Russe.

Ballet Russe

We doubt this drink had anything to do with Diaghilev himself, but are reminded that it was Diaghilev whose Ballets Russes—with its defiantly modern music, vivid colors, and bold choreography—ushered in the age of modernism in which this cocktail has flourished.

2 oz. vodka
½ oz. crème de cassis
Juice of ¼ to ½ lime

Pour ingredients into a cocktail shaker filled with ice. Shake, then strain into a chilled cocktail glass. There is an ongoing disagreement about the amount of lime juice that should go into this drink, with measures ranging from as low as a few dashes to as high as an ounce or more. It's worth making the drink a few times to discover which proportions suit you best, preferably with The Rite of Spring playing in the background.

Bardot Martini

At the Falcon Restaurant, off L.A.'s Sunset Strip, where it's a house specialty, they make this with Cîroc's Snap Frost vodka—but we advise using whatever you have on hand rather than passing up this sexy cocktail.

1 ¾ oz. vodka
1 oz. chilled orange juice
½ oz. orange liqueur
½ oz. chilled lemon-lime soda

Pour ingredients into a cocktail shaker filled with ice. Shake, then strain into a chilled cocktail glass and garnish with a twist of orange.

Bellini Martini

Though we decry the term *Martini* applied to a cocktail with so many components, the Bellini Martini can now be found on cocktail menus worldwide—and who are we to argue with a creation so delicious?

1 ½ oz. orange vodka
1 ½ oz. peach schnapps
Splash of pineapple juice
1 oz. chilled champagne

Pour vodka, schnapps, and pineapple juice into a cocktail shaker filled with ice. Shake, then strain into a chilled cocktail glass and float the champagne on top. We like this one with no garnish at all, though some add a maraschino cherry.

Black Russian

The original version of this cocktail dates back to the 1930s and paired vodka with coffee-flavored brandy. The cocktail did not become popular until the early 1960s, however, when Kahlúa was imported from Mexico to the United States for the first time and took the place of the brandy.

1 ½ oz. vodka
¾ oz. Kahlúa

Pour vodka over ice in an old fashioned glass and add Kahlúa. A garnish on a Black Russian is as out of place as the Eiffel Tower in Red Square.

FOR YOUR FURTHER DRINKING PLEASURE: If you like a sharper edge to your libations, try a **Black Magic**, made by adding a dash of freshly squeezed lemon juice and garnishing with a twist of lemon peel. Perhaps even more popular than the Black Russian is the **White Russian**, made by floating ¾ oz. cream atop a Black Russian. Flavored vodkas have further widened the possibilities. If you have a bit of a sweet tooth, try a **Raspberry Russian**, made like a White Russian with raspberry vodka and garnished with fresh raspberries, or a **Vanilla Russian**, which can be made either Black or White Russian style with vanilla vodka. And, of course, the ultimate indulgence, a **Chocolate White Russian**, made with chocolate vodka and garnished with a sprinkle of cocoa powder.

Blackberry Buck

Originally, a Buck was a cocktail of gin, ginger ale, and fruit, almost always citrus. Today, a good Buck can be made with vodka in place of gin, and a wide variety of fresh fruits, including melon, papaya, pineapple, and fresh berries. We find this version refreshing—but please feel free to make up your own combinations.

A dozen fresh blackberries, slightly crushed
¼ lemon, cut lengthwise
Dash of Angostura bitters
1 ½ oz. vodka
Chilled ginger ale

Fill a collins glass halfway with ice. Add blackberries, then fill to the top with ice. Squeeze the lemon into the glass and add bitters. Pour in vodka, then fill to the top with ginger ale and stir.

Blood Orange Lillet Cocktail

A popular cocktail at Chez Spencer in San Francisco and, now that blood oranges are often available in local stores, an excellent drink to enjoy at home.

2 ½ oz. blood orange vodka
½ oz. Lillet Blanc
Juice of ⅛ blood orange, freshly squeezed

Pour ingredients into a cocktail shaker filled with ice. Shake vigorously, then strain into a chilled cocktail glass. Garnish with a slice of blood orange.

FOR YOUR FURTHER DRINKING PLEASURE: Should you be so unfortunate as to have no blood orange vodka on hand, don't deprive yourself—mix a **Roslyn** instead. In an ice-filled shaker, combine 2 oz. each vodka and blood orange juice, add ¾ orange liqueur, and shake briskly. Strain into a chilled cocktail glass or serve over ice in an old fashioned glass.

Bloodless Mary

We found this distinctive cocktail at Dylan Prime Restaurant in New York. Although many regard it as a variation on the Bloody Mary (below), it's actually a vodka Martini.

Celery salt
2 oz. horseradish vodka

Rim a chilled cocktail glass with celery salt. Shake vodka with ice in a shaker and strain into the glass. Garnish with a thin stick of celery.

Bloody Mary

Invented at Harry's Bar in Paris in the 1920s, but Prohibition delayed the Bloody Mary's American debut until 1934, when it became a hit at the King Cole Bar in New York's St. Regis Hotel.

3 to 4 oz. tomato juice
Juice of ½ lemon
1 ½ oz. vodka
2 dashes Worcestershire sauce
Pinch of black pepper

METHOD I: Fill a highball glass almost to the top with ice. Pour in tomato juice and lemon juice. Add vodka, Worcestershire sauce, and pepper and stir.
METHOD II: Put all ingredients in a cocktail shaker filled with ice, then shake and strain into a wineglass.

FOR YOUR FURTHER DRINKING PLEASURE: The original Bloody Mary was ungarnished. Later, celery sticks, lemon, and even lime wedges became standard accompaniments. In addition to acquiring a celery swizzle stick, a contemporary Bloody Mary is also usually spiced with a dash of Tabasco sauce, a sprinkling of celery salt, or both, and a Bloody Mary made New York style will have a generous dollop of horseradish in it. An updated version of the horseradish-spiced Bloody Mary is the **Asian Mary**, in which a dollop of wasabi is added instead. We also recommend the **Bloody Bull**, in which tomato juice is replaced with a one-to-one blend of tomato juice and beef broth, and a dash of orange juice is used in place of lemon. Similar in theme is the **Bloody Caesar**, created one night at Caesar's Palace, Las Vegas, when singer Tony Bennett asked for something stabilizing. To make it, replace tomato juice with clamato (a blend of tomato and clam juices) and add generous dashes of both Tabasco sauce and celery salt. And for those who want to drink their vegetables, there's the **Gazpacho Mary**, which uses gazpacho in place of tomato juice. Finally, there's the exotic **Balsamic Morocco Mary**, which uses spicy tomato juice, lime juice instead of lemon, balsamic vinegar in place of Worcestershire sauce, and a dab of harissa instead of black pepper.

Bloody Tex-Mex

This is, of course, a variation on the Bloody Mary (see page 47), but with so many distinctive ingredients it must be made with deliberation and care.

1 ½ oz. vodka
4 to 6 oz. tomato juice
½ tsp. chili powder
¼ tsp. ground cumin
⅛ tsp. paprika
½ tsp. Worcestershire sauce
2 to 3 dashes of Tabasco sauce
¼ tsp. celery salt
Pinch of black pepper

Put ingredients in a mixing glass and stir. Pour into a large, ice-filled glass and garnish with a lime wedge or a celery stick.

Jigger Man

Cocktail Recipes
DuBOUCHETT
(Du-Bu-Shay)

Blueberry Martini

Our recipe for blueberry vodka can be found in the chapter on infusions. But if you don't have any on hand, you can get a fair approximation by mashing some berries that have been frozen and thawed, adding vodka, and letting it macerate for a few hours at room temperature.

2 oz. blueberry vodka
1 oz. raspberry liqueur
Dash of lime juice

Pour ingredients into a cocktail shaker filled with ice. Shake, then strain into a chilled cocktail glass and garnish with a few berries or a twist of lime.

Blue Hawaii

A perfect drink for a summer evening, and best drunk as the lingering twilight deepens to indigo.

1 oz. vodka
½ oz. blue curaçao
½ oz. coconut rum
2 oz. pineapple juice
Juice of 1 lime

Pour ingredients into a shaker filled with ice. Shake briskly, then strain into a chilled cocktail glass.

Blue Lagoon

Though originally made with lemon juice by its inventor, Andy MacElhone, son of Harry MacElhone of Harry's New York Bar in Paris, we offer here a more contemporary version.

1 ½ oz. vodka
½ oz. blue curaçao
Lemon-lime soda

Fill a collins glass with ice. Pour in vodka and curaçao, then fill to the rim with soda. Garnish with a slice of lemon and a cherry.

FOR YOUR FURTHER DRINKING PLEASURE: Lemonade is often used instead of soda. For the truly bold, there's also the **Blue Shark**, which uses 1 oz. tequila in place of the soda. To make this drink, shake ingredients with ice in a shaker and strain into a chilled cocktail glass.

Blue Martini

A cool, inviting cocktail to sip on a starlit night.

2 oz. vodka
1 oz. blue curaçao
Splash of dry vermouth

Pour ingredients into a cocktail shaker filled with ice. Shake briskly, then strain into a chilled cocktail glass and garnish with a twist of lemon.

Bull Shot

We like this version of the classic because, like the animal for which it's named, it has a bit of power to it. If you prefer something milder, omit the horseradish and adjust the Tabasco sauce accordingly.

1 ½ oz. vodka
4 oz. beef consommé
1 tsp. fresh lemon juice
½ tsp. grated horseradish
4 to 5 dashes of Tabasco sauce
Pinch of celery salt

Put ingredients in a large glass filled with ice, stir, and garnish with a twist of lemon.

FOR YOUR FURTHER DRINKING PLEASURE: For those who like a slightly lighter taste, we recommend a **Cock and Bull Shot**, in which equal parts of beef and chicken consommé are used, the lemon juice is increased to 1 tbsp., a single dash of Tabasco is used, and the horseradish is omitted in favor of a dash each of Worcestershire sauce and white pepper. Also worth trying is the **Gazpacho Macho**, made by using equal parts consommé and gazpacho, increasing the lemon juice to 1 tbsp., adding 1 tsp. dry sherry and a pinch of white pepper, reducing the Tabasco to a single dash, and replacing the horseradish with a dash of Worcestershire.

Buzz Bomb

"Buzz bomb" was the nickname given to the German V-1 guided missiles that rained down on London during the Blitz. Enough said?

1 oz. vodka
1 oz. cognac
1 oz. orange liqueur
1 oz. Benedictine or other herbal liqueur
Juice of 1 lime
Chilled champagne

Pour vodka, cognac, liqueurs, and lime juice into a cocktail shaker filled with ice. Shake, then strain into a tall glass and fill with champagne.

Cape Codder

In the autumn months, we like to switch to something tangy, like this venerable cocktail, forerunner to the Cosmopolitan.

1 ½ oz. vodka
Chilled cranberry juice
Dash of fresh lime juice

Pour ingredients into a highball glass filled with ice. Stir and garnish with a twist of lime.

FOR YOUR FURTHER DRINKING PLEASURE: To flaunt your vodka savvy—ask for a **Greyhound**, a highball made with vodka and grapefruit juice. Better known than the Greyhound is the **Salty Dog**, which is a Greyhound made in a glass which has been rimmed with salt.

Cherry Bomb

We came across several cocktails called the Cherry Bomb. This, based on the creation of Johnny Hernandez, of the former Patria in New York City, is one of the most complex to make—but it's well worth the effort for a special occasion.

½ oz. chocolate liqueur
¼ oz. cherry brandy
3 oz. vodka
½ oz. vanilla vodka

Several hours ahead of time, coat the inside of a cocktail glass with chocolate liqueur. Add the cherry liqueur to the center of the glass, being careful not to get any on the sides. Place in the freezer. Just before serving, pour vodkas into a cocktail shaker filled with ice, shake, then strain into the glass and garnish with a stemmed maraschino cherry or a cherry that has been marinating in chocolate liqueur. This is a potent drink, packing the jolt of love itself, and we recommend sharing it with someone dear to you.

FOR YOUR FURTHER DRINKING PLEASURE: A far simpler cocktail is the **Cherry Bomb Highball**, in which cherry vodka is mixed with cherry cola in an ice-filled glass, and garnished with a maraschino cherry.

Chi Chi

Invented in the 1950s at the Caribe Hilton Hotel in San Juan, Puerto Rico, the Piña Colada quickly became *the* signature drink of the Caribbean. Its flavors translate well to this slightly more subtle vodka version of the classic.

2 oz. vodka
1 ½ oz. cream of coconut
3 oz. chilled pineapple juice

Put ingredients in a blender with a scoop of ice. Whir and pour into a chilled hurricane or collins glass. Garnish with a spear of fresh pineapple.

FOR YOUR FURTHER DRINKING PLEASURE: Before you put the cream of coconut away, try a **Passion Chi Chi**, which is made with passion fruit juice rather than pineapple.

Chocolate Martini

There are, of course, many recipes for the Chocolate Martini. We like this one because the contrast of vodkas, paired with crème de cacao, make an intriguingly complex cocktail.

1 oz. chocolate vodka
1 oz. vanilla vodka
1 oz. dark crème de cacao

Pour ingredients into a cocktail shaker filled with ice. Shake, then strain into a chilled cocktail glass and garnish with grated chocolate.

Citronella Cooler

How to indulge our tropical dreams without abandoning our beloved vodka? The answer is here, in the Citronella Cooler.

1 oz. vodka
¼ oz. white rum
¼ oz. coconut rum
Splash of grenadine
Chilled pineapple juice

Pour vodka, rums, and grenadine into a cocktail shaker filled with ice. Shake, then strain into a collins glass filled with ice. Fill with pineapple juice and garnish with a wedge of pineapple and a maraschino cherry.

FOR YOUR FURTHER DRINKING PLEASURE: May we suggest the equally tropical **Jet Ski Jolt**? To make it, fill a collins glass with ice, pour in 1 ½ oz. each vodka, coconut rum, and grenadine, then fill with pineapple-orange-banana juice. Stir, and garnish with a maraschino cherry.

Citrus Frappe

For those dreadfully hot summer days, we recommend this icy delight.

¼ tsp. orange zest, or to taste
¼ tsp. lemon zest, or to taste
1 oz. any citrus flavored vodka
1 oz. limoncello

Fill an old fashioned glass with crushed ice. Sprinkle lemon and orange zests over ice, then pour in vodka and limoncello. Stir to mingle flavors, and garnish with a maraschino cherry.

Clementini

If you don't have clementine vodka on hand, orange may be substituted in this lovely variation on the classic vodka Martini.

2 oz. clementine vodka
Splash of dry vermouth

Pour ingredients into a cocktail shaker filled with ice. Shake vigorously, then strain into a chilled cocktail glass and garnish with a slice of clementine.

FOR YOUR FURTHER DRINKING PLEASURE: You can intensify the orange flavor of this drink by adding ¼ oz. each orange liqueur and blood orange juice.

Colony

This early vodka cocktail was a specialty of the house at New York's long gone Colony restaurant, a joint with so much cachet that Mayor Jimmy Walker had the one-way traffic on its street reversed to allow his limousine speedier access to the place.

1 ½ oz. vodka
1 oz. Southern Comfort
Juice of ½ lime

Pour ingredients into a cocktail shaker filled with ice. Shake, then strain into a chilled cocktail glass and garnish with a twist of lime.

Cosmopolitan

This classic cocktail was all the rage in the 1970s, then kept a low profile until the *Sex and the City* girls made it a hit all over again—along with several worthy variations.

1 ½ oz. vodka
1 ½ oz. cointreau
1 ½ oz. chilled cranberry juice
Juice of 1 lime

Pour ingredients into a cocktail shaker filled with ice. Shake briskly, then strain into a chilled cocktail glass and garnish with a twist of lime.

FOR YOUR FURTHER DRINKING PLEASURE: It's only natural that a cocktail this popular would inspire creative mixologists. Here are some of our favorite spin-offs, all shaken with ice and strained into a chilled cocktail glass:

COSMOPOLITAN MARTINI: 2 oz. vodka, 1 oz. orange liqueur, splash of cranberry juice, juice of ½ lime.

CRANBERRY COSMO: 2 oz. vodka, 1 oz. ginger beer, 2 tsp. thawed frozen cranberry cocktail, and pinch of ground ginger. Garnish with crystallized ginger.

DIRTY COSMOPOLITAN: An award-winning invention by Will Femia of The Slaughtered Lamb Pub in New York, this crisp cocktail uses 2 oz. citrus vodka to 1 oz. cointreau, omits the cranberry juice, and adds a splash each of fresh lime and maraschino cherry juices.

HAWAIIAN COSMO: Inspired by a drink of the same name at Jackson's Bistro in Tampa. Use equal parts pineapple vodka, chilled pineapple juice, and chilled cranberry juice. Garnish with a chunk of pineapple.

METROPOLITAN: Rapidly becoming a classic in its own right, a Metropolitan is a Cosmopolitan made with any berry-flavored vodka, such as black currant or raspberry.

PURPLE COSMO: Use 1 ½ oz. lemon vodka, then add ½ oz. each of blue curaçao, black raspberry liqueur, and Rose's lime juice. Garnish with fresh raspberries or a twist of lime.

RAZMOPOLITAN: Follow the classic Cosmopolitan recipe but use raspberry in place of plain vodka.

WHITE COSMOPOLITAN: A classic Cosmopolitan made with white cranberry juice, in which the cranberry juice and cointreau are reduced to ¾ oz. each, and a wedge of lime is used for garnish.

Crantini

Like an intense, condensed Cosmopolitan, and our favorite in November, when something crisp and refreshing fits the bill.

1 ½ oz. vodka
¾ oz. cranberry juice
½ oz. orange liqueur
½ oz. dry vermouth

Pour ingredients into a cocktail shaker filled with ice. Shake vigorously, then strain into a chilled cocktail glass. Garnish with three cranberries or a slice of orange.

Creamsicle

This sweet creation harkens back to the era of fern bars, wide ties, and mood rings, when a girl really could turn the world on with her smile.

½ oz. vodka
½ oz. orange liqueur
1 oz. chilled orange juice
1 oz. cream

Pour ingredients into a cocktail shaker filled with ice. Shake, then strain into a chilled cocktail glass.

Cucumber Gimlet

Todd Smith, of Cortez in San Francisco, infuses his own vodka for this drink. An excellent idea, and not as difficult as it sounds. Our recipe for cucumber vodka can be found on pages 127–128 of this book.

2 oz. cucumber vodka
¼ oz. simple syrup
Juice of 1 lime

Pour ingredients into a cocktail shaker filled with ice. Shake, then strain into a chilled cocktail glass and garnish with a slice of cucumber. This cocktail may also be served on the rocks in an old fashioned glass.

Cucumber Martini

A crisp yet slightly sweet cocktail, with a surprisingly sophisticated aura.

3 to 4 thin slices of cucumber
Splash of simple syrup
1 oz. vodka
1 oz. cucumber vodka

Place cucumber slices and simple syrup in a cocktail shaker and muddle thoroughly. Fill with ice, pour in vodkas, and shake to a count of 30. Strain into a chilled cocktail glass and garnish with a wheel of cucumber.

Cupid's Potion

The inventor of this drink, Julie Reiner of New York's Flatiron Lounge, uses Stolichnaya Ohranj vodka and Gran Gala orange liqueur for this cocktail. We've adapted her original for home use and beg you to try it, even if you don't have the particular brands on hand. The blood orange, however, is a must.

2 oz. orange vodka
½ oz. orange liqueur
Juice of 1 blood orange
Juice of ½ lime

Pour ingredients into a cocktail shaker filled with ice. Shake, then strain into a chilled cocktail glass and garnish with a slice of blood orange.

Czarina

A vintage drink, as one can tell from the once-preferred spelling of its name, and a preferred before-dinner drink at the now-vanished Stork Club in New York.

1 oz. vodka
¾ oz. apricot brandy
½ oz. dry vermouth
½ oz. sweet vermouth

Originally, this drink was shaken with ice in a cocktail shaker and strained into a chilled cocktail glass. We have come to prefer ours on the rocks in an old fashioned glass, garnished with a twist of lemon.

* * *

I'll picket your whole country! I'll boycott you! No more vodka! No more caviar! No more Tchaikovsky! No more borscht!

— Melvyn Douglas gets tough in *Ninotchka*, 1939

Desert Sunrise

This contemporary variation on the revered Tequila Sunrise may be even better than the drink that inspired it.

1 ½ oz. vodka
Chilled orange juice
Chilled pineapple juice
Dash of grenadine

Fill a collins glass two-thirds full with cracked ice. Pour in vodka, then fill with equal parts orange and pineapple juice. Stir once, top with grenadine, and garnish with a slice of orange.

FOR YOUR FURTHER DRINKING PLEASURE: All out of orange juice? Not to fret—follow the recipe above using all pineapple juice and you've created a **Pink Pussycat**. Another popular variation of the Desert Sunrise uses a combination of orange and apple juice in place of orange and pineapple.

WHY CRACKED ICE?

In bars, drinks like the Desert Sunrise are often served with crushed ice, usually for reasons of expediency: While crushed ice can be made by machine in large quantities, cracked ice must be made in small batches. The drawback is that crushed ice melts quickly, shortening the life of the drink and diluting its ingredients. When mixing drinks at home, we prefer cracked ice.

Devil's Torch

This is one of the very few early vodka cocktails that doesn't bear a name redolent of the Russian steppes. To the modern palate, the amount of vodka may seem insufficient. In which case, we suggest increasing the measure of vodka and decreasing the measure of vermouth.

1 ½ oz. vodka
1 ½ oz. dry vermouth
3 dashes of grenadine

Pour ingredients into a cocktail shaker filled with ice. Shake, then strain into a chilled cocktail glass and garnish with a twist of lemon peel.

FOR YOUR FURTHER DRINKING PLEASURE: A contemporary of the Devil's Torch is the **Devil's Tail**, which appears in *The Stork Club Bar Book* with the suggestion that it best be drunk on an isolated atoll in the South Pacific. To make it, replace the vermouth with the same amount of 151-proof rum, increase the grenadine to 1 oz., and add the juice of ½ lime. Whir in a blender with a scoop of ice and pour into a chilled cocktail glass.

Dillitini

Our adaptation of the invention of Dick Bradsell. Bradsell, a particularly inventive mixologist who held down the fort at Fred's Bar in London's Soho in the 1980s, is also the author of the delicious Vodka Espresso (page 107). As long as you've got the dill out, find some gravlax to go with this clean, Nordic cocktail.

Handful of fresh dill
1 ½ oz. vodka
¾ oz. aquavit

Crush the dill lightly to release its flavor, then put it with the remaining ingredients in a cocktail shaker filled with ice. Shake vigorously to a count of 25, then strain into a chilled cocktail glass.

Émigré

We think of this invention—a Balalaika with a French twist—as a kindred spirit to the Russian nobility who headed for Paris when the tsar fell. We named our creation accordingly, and have been humming ever since.

1 ½ oz. vodka
1 oz. triple sec or other orange liqueur
½ oz. cassis
Juice of ½ lime

Pour ingredients into a cocktail shaker filled with ice. Shake, then strain into a chilled cocktail glass. Because émigrés travel light, no garnish is required.

Fleur de Lis

Inspired by the sumptuous original drink, as served at the wonderful Roech restaurant in Boston.

1 ½ oz. raspberry vodka
1 oz. orange liqueur
Splash of sweet and sour mix
Splash of Rose's lime juice

Pour ingredients into a cocktail shaker filled with ice. Shake, then strain into a chilled cocktail glass and garnish with a twist of lime.

Flying Fortress

Now that absinthe has been reimagined in a form that's safe, this World War II–era cocktail can be made as originally intended.

1 ½ oz. brandy
1 oz. vodka
¾ oz. orange liqueur
¾ oz. Absente

Pour ingredients into a cocktail shaker filled with ice. Shake briskly, then strain into a chilled cocktail glass and garnish with a slice of orange.

French Kiss

Like the kiss for which it is named, this is a sweet caress that leaves you wanting more. But beware: Too many of them will leave your head spinning.

1 ½ oz. vodka
½ oz. raspberry liqueur
2 oz. chilled pineapple juice

Pour ingredients into a cocktail shaker filled with ice. Shake, then strain into a chilled cocktail glass and garnish with a cube of pineapple.

French Vanilla Swirl

What happens in Vegas shouldn't always stay in Vegas. This is our adaptation of the cocktail created by Rodney Kettler of the Piero Selvaggio Valentino.

1 ½ oz. vanilla vodka
¾ oz. black raspberry liqueur
¾ oz. pineapple juice
¾ oz. sweet and sour mix

Pour ingredients into a cocktail shaker filled with ice. Shake briskly, then strain into a chilled cocktail glass and garnish with fresh raspberries or a wedge of pineapple.

Georgia Peach

If lemonade drinks remind you of the disastrous cocktails of your youth, try this gossamer refresher.

2 oz. vodka
1 oz. peach schnapps
½ oz. grenadine
Chilled lemonade

Pour vodka, schnapps, and grenadine into a highball glass two thirds full of ice cubes. Fill with lemonade, stir, and garnish with a slice of lemon.

Gimlet

Though the original Gimlet is a gin drink, friends on both sides of the bar now tell us that the vodka Gimlet has surpassed it in popularity.

1 ½ oz. vodka
½ oz. Rose's lime juice

Pour ingredients into an old fashioned glass filled with ice. Stir, and garnish with a wedge of lime. Note that the drink can also be served straight up: Shake the ingredients in a cocktail shaker filled with ice, strain into a chilled cocktail glass, and garnish with a twist of lime.

Ginger Martini

Don't be put off by the fact that this calls for ginger syrup. It's easy to make, and our recipe is in the Here's How section on page 35.

3 oz. vodka

1 oz. ginger syrup

Juice of ¼ lime

Pour ingredients into a cocktail shaker filled with ice. Shake to a count of 30, then strain into a chilled cocktail glass and garnish with candied ginger or a twist of lime peel.

FOR YOUR FURTHER DRINKING PLEASURE: As long as you've got the ginger syrup out, try a **Ginger-Lime Martini**. Use 3 oz. lime vodka, the juice of 1 lime, a splash of orange liqueur, and garnish with a wedge of lime.

Gingersnap

If you have ginger liqueur around, by all means use it. But as it's a somewhat exotic ingredient, we've fashioned our recipe with the ginger syrup whose recipe can be found on page 35 of this book.

1 ½ oz. orange vodka
Splash of ginger syrup
Chilled champagne

Pour vodka and syrup into a cocktail shaker filled with ice. Shake, then strain into a chilled cocktail glass and fill with champagne.

Glögg

Not many vodka drinks are served hot, but this sweetly spiced Scandinavian punch is a wintertime tradition well worth preserving.

½ tsp. crushed cardamom seeds
2 cinnamon sticks
6 cloves
2 tbsp. honey
¼ vanilla bean
1 (750ml) bottle red wine
½ c. vodka
½ c. almonds, blanched
¼ c. golden raisins
Orange slices

In a medium saucepan, bring 1 cup water to a boil. Add cardamom, cinnamon, cloves, honey, and vanilla bean. Reduce heat and simmer gently 15 minutes. In a larger pot, gently warm the wine. Add half of the spice-infused water and taste. Add more until you reach the level of sweetness preferred. Add vodka, almonds, and raisins. Place a slice of orange in each cup and ladle in the glögg.

Godmother

A variation of the Godfather, which is made with scotch and amaretto, this crisp spouse of the original is well worth a try.

1 ½ oz. vodka
¾ oz. amaretto

Fill an old fashioned glass with ice. Pour in vodka, then amaretto and stir. Garnish with a long spiral of lemon zest.

Golden Martini

This drink is the creation of Armando Rosario of the former Le Cirque 2000 in New York. The master mixologist recommends Rain vodka for the main ingredient.

4 oz. vodka
1 oz. sauterne

Pour ingredients into a cocktail shaker filled with ice. Shake, then strain into a chilled cocktail glass and garnish with three white grapes.

Grapetini

At Hollywood's Vert Restaurant, where this is a signature drink, Chef Wolfgang Puck uses Cîroc's Snap Frost vodka and Moët & Chandon champagne for this cocktail. Excellent choices, which we heartily endorse.

1 ½ oz. vodka
1 oz. chilled white grape juice
½ oz. chilled champagne

Rim a chilled cocktail glass with superfine sugar. Pour vodka and grape juice into a cocktail shaker filled with ice. Shake, then strain into the prepared glass. Add champagne and garnish with a frozen white or green grape.

Hairy Navel

A variation on the Fuzzy Navel, that whimsically named cocktail from the funkadelic '70s.

1 ½ oz. vodka
¾ oz. peach schnapps
Chilled cranberry juice

Pour vodka and schnapps over ice in a highball glass, top with cranberry juice and stir.

FOR YOUR FURTHER DRINKING PLEASURE: A drink that actually predates the Hairy Navel is the **Firefly**: Combine 1 oz. each of vodka and peach schnapps in a highball glass with ice, stir, then fill with chilled orange juice.

Harvey Wallbanger

This long, tall version of a Screwdriver can be quite captivating, but beware: The sweet touch of Galliano makes the drink go down a little too smoothly, leading to swift inebriation—as Harvey (whoever he was) apparently found out.

1 ½ oz. vodka
Chilled orange juice
1 tbsp. Galliano

Fill a collins glass with ice. Add vodka, then fill almost to the top with orange juice and float the Galliano on top.

Hawaiian Lime Squeeze

We once discovered this delightfully simple cocktail at the bar of the Kahala Mandarin Oriental Hotel in Hawaii. Fatigued by an exhaustive day of research, we found ourselves instantly restored and feeling as fresh as an island breeze after just one sip. The drink quickly became our favorite, and remained so long after our final alohas were said.

2 oz. vodka
1 oz. triple sec
Juice of ½ lime
Dash of Rose's lime juice

Pour ingredients into a cocktail shaker filled with ice. Shake briskly, then strain into an old fashioned glass half-filled with ice cubes. Garnish with a good-sized wedge of lime.

Honey Girl

On Hawaii, "honey girl" denotes a young lady who's sweet and a little bit sassy. This 1990s cocktail was purportedly created by a Maui bartender in honor of his hula-dancer girlfriend, who was every bit a honey girl. Note that this recipe makes two cocktails, so plan on sharing it with your honey.

3 oz. vodka
⅓ c. guava nectar
⅓ c. pineapple juice
¼ c. frozen strawberries and syrup, thawed and pureed

Pour ingredients into a cocktail shaker filled with ice. Shake, then pour into two chilled cocktail glasses and garnish each with a fresh strawberry.

Iced Teani

Thoroughly refreshing, and the variations are endless.

2 oz. vodka
1 oz. cooled tea

Pour ingredients into a cocktail shaker filled with ice. Shake briskly, then strain into a chilled cocktail glass and garnish with a twist of lemon and a sprig of fresh mint.

FOR YOUR FURTHER DRINKING PLEASURE: Experiment using your favorite flavors of tea. We're especially fond of peach green tea in this, and of raspberry. Our only caveat is to avoid prepared teas or mixes that have been sweetened.

Kamikaze

This beautifully simple, easy-to-remember recipe delivers, as the name suggests, a swift and direct strike.

1 oz. vodka
1 oz. triple sec
Juice of 1 lime

Pour ingredients into a cocktail shaker filled with ice and shake briskly. This drink is equally good straight up or on the rocks, so depending on your whim, strain into a chilled cocktail glass or into an old fashioned glass filled with ice.

Key Lime Martini

We never fail to make this cocktail whenever key limes are in season. The vanilla vodka provides a nice balance for the acidic limes.

1 ½ oz. vanilla vodka
1 oz. pineapple juice
¾ oz. fresh key lime juice
Splash of simple syrup

Pour ingredients into a cocktail shaker filled with ice. Shake vigorously, then strain into a chilled cocktail glass and garnish with a wheel of key lime.

FOR YOUR FURTHER DRINKING PLEASURE: When served at the Grand Café at the Hotel Monaco in San Francisco, a splash of cointreau is used in place of simple syrup.

Kumquatini

Shortly after this cocktail became a popular signature drink at the City Hall Restaurant in New York, previously rare kumquats became available all over Manhattan. Coincidence? We think not.

2 oz. orange vodka
1 oz. vanilla vodka
1 oz. orange liqueur
Splash of orange juice

Pour ingredients into a cocktail shaker filled with ice. Shake, then strain into a chilled champagne glass and garnish with a wheel of kumquat.

Lemon Cassis Martini

A perfect cocktail for those last days of winter when it seems spring will never come, this drink brims with the promise of berries ripening in the sun.

3 oz. lemon vodka
1 tbsp. sweet and sour mix
1 tbsp. cassis

Pour ingredients into a cocktail shaker filled with ice. Shake until very cold, then strain into a chilled cocktail glass and garnish with a twist of lemon.

Lemon Drop

We used to dismiss this cocktail as rather ho-hum—until we tried it with lemon vodka.

1 ½ oz. lemon vodka
Juice of 1 small lemon
1 tsp. superfine sugar

Pour ingredients into a cocktail shaker filled with ice. Shake until the sugar is dissolved, then strain into a chilled cocktail glass and garnish with a slice of lemon.
FOR YOUR FURTHER DRINKING PLEASURE: We also recommend the **Watermelon Drop**, which is made with vanilla vodka, lemon juice, and, in place of the sugar, 1 oz. watermelon schnapps.

Limoncello Spritzer

If you've never made your own limoncello, you're missing out. Try our recipe for this lemony vodka liqueur, found on pages 137–138 of this book.

4 oz. limoncello
2 oz. chilled club soda
Juice of ¼ to ½ lime, or to taste

Fill a collins glass with ice. Pour in limoncello, club soda, and lime juice. Stir, add more ice if needed, and garnish with a wedge of lemon or lime.

Lychee Martini

Like the Appletini, this variation on a vodka Martini has become a contemporary classic, with as many different recipes as there are establishments serving it. Lychee liqueur is often called for, but for those who don't stock such exotic ingredients, we offer this simpler recipe.

2 oz. vodka
1 oz. syrup from canned lychees

Place 1 or 2 canned lychees in a chilled cocktail glass. Pour vodka and syrup into a cocktail shaker filled with ice. Shake briskly, then strain into the glass.

FOR YOUR FURTHER DRINKING PLEASURE: Use ginger-infused vodka (see page 128), or add a pinch of powdered or freshly grated ginger, for a **Lychee Ginger Martini**. Some people also like to add a few drops of grenadine to give this cocktail the ruby glow of fresh lychees. We have also encountered a lovely drink called the **Lotus Flower**, which is made like the Lychee Martini but uses orange vodka and, in addition to the lychee syrup, adds 2 tsp. pink grapefruit juice, a dash of orange bitters, and 2 dashes of sweet and sour mix.

Mango Mimosa Martini

On a research expedition to Grand Cayman, we discovered this creation of the Reef Grill on Seven Mile Beach.

1 ½ oz. vodka
1 ½ oz. mango mix, such as Rose's Mango Twist
1 ½ oz. chilled champagne

Pour vodka and mango mix into a cocktail shaker filled with ice. Shake briskly, then strain into a chilled cocktail glass and top with champagne. Garnish with a twist of orange and a cube of fresh mango.

Mango Sour

2 oz. vodka
3 oz. mango nectar
Juice of 1 small lemon
2 tsp. superfine sugar

Pour ingredients into a cocktail shaker filled with ice. Shake to a count of 30, then strain into a double old fashioned glass half-filled with ice. Garnish with a spear of mango.

Martini

Without doubt, the Martini is the single most famous cocktail of all time. Though originally a gin drink, today's drinkers often prefer theirs, like Agent 007, with vodka. Modern taste buds also prefer a drink that is relatively dry —whereas the original cocktail called for equal amounts of gin and vermouth, vermouth these days is more essence than actuality.

Dry Martini

3 oz. vodka
1 tbsp. dry vermouth

Pour ingredients into a cocktail shaker filled with ice. Shake until too cold to handle, then strain into a chilled cocktail glass and garnish with an olive.

Very Dry Martini

3 oz. vodka
1 tsp. (or less) dry vermouth

Pour ingredients into a cocktail shaker filled with ice. Shake until too cold to handle, then strain into a chilled cocktail glass and garnish with an olive.

FOR YOUR FURTHER DRINKING PLEASURE: There are hundreds of variations on the vodka Martini, ranging from excellent to dreadful and from genuine

Martinis to Martinis in name only. We've listed the best of the fanciful ones under their own names, and our favorite true-to-the-originals below.

BASIL MARTINI: A Dry Martini made with basil-infused vodka (see page 128) and with 1 tbsp. spiced tomato mix or Bloody Mary mix replacing the vermouth. Garnish with a cherry tomato, or a thin slice of dried tomato (not oil-packed).

BUCKEYE MARTINI: A Martini garnished with a black, rather than green, olive.

CAJUN MARTINI: Also known as a Chili or Pepper Martini. Made according to the recipe for a Dry Martini, above, with chili pepper vodka and garnished with a thin slice of jalapeño.

DIRTY MARTINI: A Very Dry Martini to which a few drops of green olive brine have been added.

ROSEMARINO: A signature cocktail at New York's Gramercy Tavern, this is a Martini made with rosemary-infused vodka (see page 128) and garnished with capers.

SILVER BULLET: There are several versions of this drink, but one of the best is a vodka Martini with a hint of scotch. To prepare, follow the directions for the Dry Martini, on page 82, but add 1 tsp. of scotch to the shaker. Garnish with a twist of lemon peel.

TOMOLIVE MARTINI: One of our all-time favorites, also known at Jane in New York as a Dirty Jane. To 2 parts vodka, add 1 part brine from pickled green tomatoes and forget the vermouth completely. Garnish with a thin slice of pickled tomato.

Melon Ball

Midori created this cocktail to introduce their melon liqueur to the United States. It was love at first sight, and the drink has been a classic ever since.

1 oz. vodka
2 oz. melon liqueur
Chilled pineapple juice

Combine vodka and melon liqueur in a collins glass filled with ice. Fill with pineapple juice and garnish with a chunk of pineapple.

Mexitini

The degree of warmth in this cocktail is up to you and the pepper sauce. We like ours medium, with the blending warmth of cumin.

3 oz. vodka
Dash of dry vermouth
Dashes of your favorite jalapeño pepper sauce, to taste
Pinch of ground cumin

Pour ingredients into a cocktail shaker filled with ice. Shake, then strain into a chilled cocktail glass and garnish with a jalapeño-stuffed olive, a slice of pickled okra, or a spiced pickled green bean.

FOR YOUR FURTHER DRINKING PLEASURE: A dash of orange bitters can add an interesting top note to this cocktail.

Moscow Mule

Though the invention of this cocktail is frequently traced to 1962 and a bartender at the Cock 'n Bull in Hollywood, it appeared in Harry Craddock's *Savoy Cocktail Book* as early as 1930. Most likely it was the Cock 'n Bull bartender who retrieved it from obscurity, for the drink did not become widely popular until the atomic era.

1 ½ oz. vodka
½ lime, cut lengthwise into 4 wedges
Ginger beer

Fill a mug or collins glass with ice and add vodka. Squeeze lime into the glass and drop in the squeezed wedges. Fill to the top with ginger beer. Those who prefer a kickier mule may add a few drops of Angostura bitters. Note that the Moscow Mule as described by Lucius Beebe, author of *The Stork Club Bar Book*, was garnished with fresh mint.

FOR YOUR FURTHER DRINKING PLEASURE: For those who like a little more heat, we recommend the **Peppered Mule**, made with spicy pepper vodka. Another delightful variation is the **Ginger Seville**, in which orange vodka is used in place of the original plain. Follow the method above but use ginger ale in place of beer and you will have a refreshing **Vodka Chiller**.

Our rule: the hotter the day, the more lime.

Mudslide

Forget dessert—serve this instead.

Hot brewed coffee
1 oz. vodka
1 oz. Irish cream liqueur
1 scoop of ice cream

Fill a mug two-thirds full of coffee. Add vodka and liqueur, top with ice cream, and stir.

Orange Martini

When we crave something that's simple to make yet tastes complex, we turn to this recipe.

3 oz. vodka
½ oz. orange liqueur
Dash of orange bitters

Pour ingredients into a cocktail shaker filled with ice. Shake until too cold to handle, then strain into a chilled cocktail glass and garnish with a twist of orange.

Orange Mist

A slightly more potent variation on the Screwdriver. Unconventional and definitely worth trying.

1 oz. vodka
1 oz. Irish whiskey
2 oz. orange juice
Chilled club soda

Pour vodka, whiskey, and orange juice into a cocktail shaker filled with ice. Shake vigorously, then pour into a large chilled collins glass, fill with soda, and garnish with a slice of orange and a maraschino cherry.

Peach Sally

A fter failing to find our favorite peach blossom tea for sale, we decamped to a favorite watering hole and, with the help of a talented bar chef, invented this delightful substitute.

2 oz. peach vodka
1 oz. chilled champagne

The ingredients can either be gently stirred with ice in a mixing glass and strained into a chilled cocktail glass or served on the rocks in an old fashioned glass. In either case, it's best garnished with a slice of fresh freestone peach.

Peach Sangria

Everyone should have one good, sophisticated sangria recipe in their repertoire. This is ours.

1 (750ml) bottle white wine
¾ c. peach vodka
1 lb. peaches, pitted and sliced
¾ c. cherries, pitted and halved
¾ c. mangos, cubed
1 c. chilled ginger ale

In a large pitcher, combine wine, vodka, and fruits and refrigerate until thoroughly chilled, at least three hours or overnight. Just before serving, add ginger ale. Serve over ice, being sure to include a few pieces of fruit in each glass.

Pear Martini

Who would know better how to mix a perfect Pear Martini? The Martini Bar in Miami's South Beach offers this deliciously simple answer.

3 oz. vodka
1 oz. pear liqueur

Pour ingredients into a cocktail shaker filled with ice. Stir, then strain into a chilled cocktail glass and garnish with frozen green grapes.

Persephone's Kiss

We think scarlet-hued, sweet-tart, slightly exotic pomegranate juice makes the perfect cocktail on Valentine's Day—but we confess, we like this creation so much we drink it year round.

2 oz. vodka

2 oz. chilled pomegranate juice

Place several ice cubes in an old fashioned glass. Add vodka and pomegranate juice and stir.

FOR YOUR FURTHER DRINKING PLEASURE: Proving that great minds think alike, we discovered a similar cocktail at Pravda in New York City. We cloned the bar's **Pomegranate Martini** by pouring 1 ½ oz. vodka, 1 ½ oz. pomegranate juice, and 1 tsp. simple syrup into a cocktail shaker filled with ice, then shaking and straining into a chilled cocktail glass.

Pineappletini

Y ou can never be too rich or too sophisticated, as this cocktail proves.

1 ½ oz. pineapple vodka
½ oz. vanilla vodka
2 oz. pineapple juice
Splash of cream

Pour ingredients into a cocktail shaker filled with ice. Shake vigorously, then strain into a chilled cocktail glass and garnish with a chunk of pineapple.

FOR YOUR FURTHER DRINKING PLEASURE: If you prefer your drinks without dairy, susbstitute a splash of grenadine for the cream.

Pineapple Cooler

W hen you want something long, tall, and refreshing, try this—and break out the paper umbrellas.

1 oz. pineapple vodka
1 oz. raspberry vodka
½ oz. melon liqueur
Splash of grenadine
Chilled pineapple juice

Fill a collins glass with ice. Add vodkas, liqueur, and grenadine. Stir, then fill almost to the top with pineapple juice. Add a fruit festival of garnishes: pineapple spear, orange wheel, and maraschino cherry.

Pink Sink

Inspired by a drink of the same name as served at the Hi-Life Restaurant in Seattle. For us, this deceptively simple drink was love at first sip.

2 oz. black currant vodka
¾ oz. peach schnapps
Juice of ½ lemon

Pour ingredients into a cocktail shaker filled with ice. Shake, then strain into a chilled cocktail glass.

Pink Squirrel

Many dismiss the Pink Squirrel as a gimmicky drink, mild and sweet and frequently made with ice cream. Keep an open mind, and try this more balanced version.

1 oz. vodka
1 oz. crème de noyaux
½ oz. white crème de cacao
½ oz. cream

Pour ingredients into a cocktail shaker filled with ice. Shake, then strain into a chilled cocktail glass. You may use another almond liqueur in place of crème de noyaux, but if you do, add a dash of maraschino cherry juice to achieve this cocktail's classic pink hue.

Purple Haze

Part of the fun of making this drink is watching the ingredients mingle to purple. Sip it on a summer afternoon, just as the first deep shadows are falling.

2 oz. cranberry vodka
2 oz. cranberry juice
½ oz. blue curaçao
1 scant tsp. Rose's lime juice
Chilled lemon-lime soda

Pour vodka, cranberry juice, curaçao, and Rose's lime juice over ice in a collins glass. Top with soda, stir, garnish with a twist of lemon, and serve with a straw.

Red Party

Of the Communists of old had made this their house drink, we think the Party would still be going on.

1 ½ oz. vodka
½ oz. black raspberry liqueur
6 raspberries, mashed to puree
1 scant tbsp. heavy cream

Put vodka, liqueur, and raspberries in a cocktail shaker filled with ice. Shake, then strain into a chilled cocktail glass. Float cream on top.

FOR YOUR FURTHER DRINKING PLEASURE: A good example of how the personality of a drink can change dramatically with a minimal alteration of ingredients is a drink we call the **Midsummer Smile**, in honor of the longest day of the year, when berries are slowly ripening in the sun. Make it as you would a Red Party, replacing the mashed raspberries with the juice of ½ lemon, and topping the drink with a float of champagne rather than cream.

Reindeer Martini

Our version of the drink of the same name served at Harry's Velvet Room in Chicago, where mixologist Sherri Flynn, who created it, recommends using Rain vodka, Frangelico, and Malibu rum.

2 oz. vodka
1 oz. hazelnut liqueur
1 oz. coconut rum
Splash of light cream

Pour ingredients into a cocktail shaker filled with ice. Shake vigorously, then strain into a chilled cocktail glass and garnish with Rudolph's red nose of a maraschino cherry and two cinnamon stick antlers.

Service with Charm!

Screaming Orgasm

From the era when free love reigned, and even nice girls asked for exactly what they wanted.

1 oz. vodka
1 oz. Irish cream liqueur
1 oz. coffee liqueur
1 oz. almond liqueur

Pour ingredients into a cocktail shaker filled with ice. Shake, then strain into a chilled cocktail glass

FOR YOUR FURTHER DRINKING PLEASURE: If you don't mind making a bit of noise, may we suggest a **Multiple Orgasm**? Follow the recipe above but reduce all four ingredients to ½ oz. each and add 2 oz. light cream or half-and-half.

✳ ✳ ✳

I will not be defeated by a bad man and an American stick insect. Instead, I choose vodka.

— Renée Zellweger chooses sides in *Bridget Jones' Diary*, 2001

Screwdriver

The most famous of all vodka highballs, the Screwdriver earned its name the old-fashioned way—when an engineer used the gadget to stir some vodka into his orange juice.

1 ½ oz. vodka
Chilled orange juice

Pour vodka, then orange juice into a highball glass filled with ice. Stir, then garnish with a slice of orange.

FOR YOUR FURTHER DRINKING PLEASURE: It didn't take long for the double entendre bunch to come up with titillating innovations, starting with a **Comfortable Screw**, in which the vodka is reduced to 1 oz. and 1 oz. Southern Comfort is added. Then there's the **Slow Comfortable Screw**, in which the orange juice is mixed with ¾ oz. each of vodka, sloe gin, and Southern Comfort.

A simpler—and less embarrassing—drink to request is a **Green Eyes**, which is a Screwdriver with ¾ oz. blue curaçao added.

Sea Breeze

One sip of this refreshing classic and you'll see the brilliance in its name—it's tart, and as bracing as an afternoon at full sail.

1 ½ oz. vodka
Chilled grapefruit juice
Chilled cranberry juice

Place a generous amount of ice in a highball glass. Pour in vodka, then fill with equal parts grapefruit and cranberry juices.

FOR YOUR FURTHER DRINKING PLEASURE: Equally delicious and lovely to behold is the **Madras**, made exactly like a Sea Breeze but with orange juice instead of grapefruit. And for those who'd like to stay closer to shore, there's the congenial **Bay Breeze**, made with the same amount of vodka and a mix of two-thirds pineapple juice and one-third cranberry juice. And if you use equal parts pineapple and cranberry juice, your drink is a **Downeaster**.

Sex on the Beach

1 oz. vodka
1 oz. peach schnapps
Chilled orange juice
Chilled cranberry juice

Place several ice cubes in a collins glass. Add vodka and schnapps, then fill to the top with equal parts orange and cranberry juice and garnish with a slice of orange.

FOR YOUR FURTHER DRINKING PLEASURE: If you strip off the fruit juices, you're right down to a **Silk Panties** cocktail. Pour the vodka and schnapps into a cocktail shaker with ice, then strain into a cocktail glass filled with cracked ice.

Snow White

Actress Bonita Granville, who played teen sleuth Nancy Drew in a series of 1930s movies, described this as the bartender's answer to the atomic bomb. We don't disagree.

5 oz. Southern Comfort
1 oz. vodka
1 oz. chilled pineapple juice
½ oz. chilled orange juice

Place ingredients in a blender along with a scoop of ice. Whir to slush, pour into a double old fashioned glass, and garnish with a maraschino cherry. Serve with a compass so you can find your way home.

Sorbet Cocktail

The fun of this cocktail is mixing and matching your favorite sorbets with your favorite flavored vodkas.

1 c. chilled sparkling white wine
1 oz. iced vodka
2 or 3 small scoops frozen sorbet

Pour wine and vodka into a chilled wineglass or champagne flute. Gently add sorbet and serve immediately.

✳ ✳ ✳

Well, Dave, yeah. It's true. I am a vegetarian. But I hear that vodka comes from a potato!

– Bette Midler stands her ground in *Down and Out in Beverly Hills*, 1986

Stoli Around the World

There's always some daredevil who wants to fly around the world. In this case, a whole lot of daredevils—we're told that this is one of the most popular vodka drinks of the new millennium.

½ oz. of each of Stolichnaya's fruit vodkas: orange, raspberry, cranberry, strawberry, peach, and citrus
1 oz. chilled cranberry juice
1 oz. chilled pineapple juice
Splash of lemon-lime soda

Pour ingredients into a cocktail shaker filled with ice. Shake until shaker is very cold, then strain into a very large chilled cocktail glass or chilled old fashioned glass. This drink can also be served over ice in a tall collins glass. Garnish with a slice of orange.

Strawberry Cooler

Actually, this concept and method work for a wide variety of fruit and fruit syrups. In addition to strawberry, we're especially fond of blueberry, lemon, lime, and passion fruit.

Fresh strawberries
1 ½ oz. vodka
1 oz. strawberry syrup
Dash of fresh lemon juice
Chilled club soda

Muddle 2 or 3 berries in an old fashioned or collins glass. Fill glass with ice and set aside. Pour vodka, syrup, and lemon juice into a cocktail shaker filled with ice. Shake vigorously, then strain into prepared glass. Fill with soda and garnish with a fresh berry.

Summer Slush

Sometimes, happiness is in your own backyard. We tried many slush recipes and found them all too sweet. Then a relative handed us her recipe, which we adjusted slightly. We love this for a summer party, since you can make it up ahead of time.

4 green tea bags (we like the peach flavored variety)
2 c. sugar
1 (12oz) can frozen orange juice concentrate, thawed
1 (12oz) can frozen limeade concentrate, thawed
1 c. vodka

Bring 2 cups water to a boil. Add tea bags, steep for a minimum of 5 minutes, remove the tea bags, and set tea aside to cool.

In a large pot, bring 7 cups water to a boil. Lower the heat and add sugar. Stir until completely dissolved, then let cool to room temperature.

Combine tea, sweetened water, and concentrates and mix thoroughly. Place in one large or two smaller plastic containers with lids and place in freezer. Stir thoroughly every 5 hours.

The next day, stir in vodka. Freeze for 3 to 5 more hours.

To serve, scoop into glasses and serve with spoons and straws.

FOR YOUR FURTHER DRINKING PLEASURE: If you're making this for a party that will be attended by nondrinkers, make a second batch but omit the vodka. To make sure no one picks up the wrong drink by mistake, we strongly recommend coloring this **Virgin Slush** with grenadine.

Sunset Martini

●nspired by a drink of the same name served at the Old Fort Pub in Hilton Head, South Carolina. There's nothing Martini-ish about it, but we promise it will summon the memory of sunlight, blue waves, and sails billowing with summer breezes.

1 ½ oz. raspberry vodka
2 oz. pineapple juice
Dash of orange liqueur
Dash of grenadine

Pour ingredients into a cocktail shaker filled with ice. Shake, then strain into a chilled cocktail glass and garnish with a cube of pineapple.

Tatanka

●n the middle of the first decade of the new millennium, this was the #1 vodka drink in Europe, rocking taste buds from Krakow to Knightsbridge. Tatanka, Lakota for "buffalo," can be attributed to the vodka most often called for, Zubrowka, a Polish vodka made from buffalo grass.

1 ½ oz. vodka
Chilled apple juice

Fill a collins glass with several cubes of ice. Pour in vodka, then apple juice, and garnish with a slice of green apple.

FOR YOUR FURTHER DRINKING PLEASURE: Made with a citron flavored vodka, this drink is known as a **Vincent Vega**.

Tovarich

A drink from the late 1930s, when one wouldn't dream of giving a vodka cocktail anything *but* a Russian name. In this case, the appellation most likely comes from the 1937 movie of the same name, starring those two oh-so-Russian thespians, Claudette Colbert and Charles Boyer.

2 oz. vodka
1 ½ oz. kümmel
Juice of ½ lime

Pour ingredients into a cocktail shaker filled with ice. Shake briskly, then strain into a chilled cocktail glass.

menu

Vesper

This drink first appears in *Casino Royale*, the first of the James Bond books. It's named for the story's beautifully blond double agent, played by Ursula Andress in the movie. The proportions are devilish, but well worth the effort.

2 oz. gin
1 tbsp. plus 1 tsp. vodka
2 tsp. blonde Lillet

Pour ingredients into a cocktail shaker filled with ice. Shake, then strain into a chilled cocktail glass and garnish with a twist of lemon peel.

✳ ✳ ✳

"A dry Martini," he said. "One.
In a deep champagne goblet."
"Oui, Monsieur."
"Just a moment. Three measures of Gordon's, one of vodka,
half a measure of Kina Lillet. Shake it very well until
it's ice-cold, then add a large slice of lemon-peel. Got it?"

— *Casino Royale*, by Ian Fleming

Vodka Collins

This is a fine drink if you avoid the tempting faux pas of reaching for that odious invention known as Collins Mixer. Fresh ingredients, please!

2 oz. vodka
Juice of ½ lemon
1 tsp. superfine sugar
Chilled club soda

Put vodka, lemon juice, and sugar in a mixing glass filled with ice and stir to dissolve sugar. Strain into a collins glass filled with ice cubes. Add soda and garnish with a lemon slice and a maraschino cherry.

FOR YOUR FURTHER DRINKING PLEAS- URE: If you have citrus vodkas on hand, try a collins with a twist. A **Lime Vodka Collins**, garnished with a wedge of lime, is particularly refreshing on a hot afternoon, while those who want a very astringent cocktail will thrill to a **Grapefruit Vodka Collins**. For those who crave a slightly sweeter drink, try a **Berry Collins**, made with the berry-flavored vodka of your choice and all the better if you begin by muddling a few fresh berries in the bottom of the collins glass.

Vodka Cooler

We save this one for the hottest of summer days, when something both crisp and cooling is called for.

3 oz. citrus vodka
3/4 oz. orange liqueur
Juice of 1 1/2 limes

Pour ingredients into a cocktail shaker filled with ice. Shake until cold as a Minnesota winter, then pour into an old fashioned glass filled with ice and garnish with a wedge of lime.

Vodka Espresso

According to legend, this 1980s cocktail was invented in a Soho, London bar one night when a famous model asked for something that would wake her up, then shake her up. Only the word she used instead of *shake* was a good deal ruder—in contrast to the wonderfully smooth drink.

1 1/2 oz. vodka
1 1/2 oz. espresso
Dash of simple syrup
Dash of coffee liqueur

Pour ingredients into a cocktail shaker filled with ice. Shake, then strain into a chilled cocktail glass. If you have roasted espresso beans on hand, drop 3 into the glass as a garnish.

Vodka Highball

Technically, any combination of vodka and a mixer would fit the definition "highball." But leave it to master mixologist Dale DeGroff to come up with this sophisticated combination.

1 ½ oz. vodka
Juice of ½ lime
2 dashes of Angostura bitters
Ginger ale

Pour ingredients into a highball glass filled with ice. Stir and garnish with a twist of lime.

FOR YOUR FURTHER DRINKING PLEASURE: While we're on the highball trail, may we suggest the **Vodka 7** ? To make it, simply omit the bitters and replace ginger ale with your favorite lemon-lime soda.

Vodka Rickey

What could possibly be more refreshing on a summer evening? In our view, nothing.

1 ½ oz. vodka
Juice of 1 lime
Club soda

Fill a collins glass with ice. Add ingredients, stir, and garnish with a wedge of lime.

FOR YOUR FURTHER DRINKING PLEASURE: Rickeys were popular throughout the 1930s and '40s and, frankly, we think it's time for the rickey concept to make a big comeback. Any flavored or infused vodka that goes well with citrus will make an intriguing rickey, including lime, orange, grapefruit, and our current favorite, raspberry.

club
hollywood
ROCKY HILL   CONNECTICUT

Vodka Sling

Today, people equate tropical drinks with rum. But one of the best, invented almost a century ago at the Raffles Hotel and named for the city of its origin, contained gin. We're happy to report that the famous Singapore Sling is even more delicious made with vodka.

1 lime
1 oz. vodka
1 oz. cherry brandy
1 oz. Benedictine
Chilled club soda

Using a zester or paring knife, remove peel from lime in a long, continuous spiral and set aside. Pour vodka, brandy, and Benedictine into a cocktail shaker filled with ice. Shake, then strain into a tall collins glass filled with ice. Fill with soda and add the entire lime peel.

FOR YOUR FURTHER DRINKING PLEASURE: In many ports of the Pacific, ginger ale rather than club soda is the preferred mixer for a sling. If you like a slightly sharper edge to your cocktail, we recommend a **Straits Sling** made with vodka. Follow the recipe above, adding to your cocktail shaker the juice of ½ lemon and 1 or 2 dashes of either orange or Angostura bitters.

Vodka Sour

Most sour recipes call for lemon juice only. But in this one, we like the complexity of both lemon and lime.

2 oz. vodka
2 tbsp. simple syrup, or to taste
Juice of 1 lemon
Juice of 1 lime

Pour ingredients into a cocktail shaker filled with ice. Shake, then strain into a chilled cocktail glass and garnish with a maraschino cherry.

FOR YOUR FURTHER DRINKING PLEASURE: For a more intense taste, try this drink with citrus, lemon, lime, or red grapefruit vodka.

Vodka Stinger

According to those who know, the Stinger is the traditional New York nightcap. No matter which way your evening went, this treat makes the whole day seem worthwhile.

1 ½ oz. vodka
¾ oz. white crème de menthe

The traditional way to make a Stinger is to rumble the ingredients in a shaker filled with ice and strain into a chilled cocktail glass. Modern sippers, however, often prefer the spirits poured over ice in an old fashioned glass and stirred.

Vodka & Tonic

The key to a spectacular version of this highball lies in the preparation. Starting with well-chilled vodka and tonic water and taking time to gloss the glass with lime will make all the difference.

1 ½ oz. vodka
Chilled tonic water

Rub the rim of a highball glass with a wedge of lime. Fill glass with ice, add vodka, fill with tonic water, and garnish with a wedge of lime.

Vodkaccino

Vodka, coffee, and chocolate are natural soul mates. Add a touch of cream and you have divine inspiration—for the hot months of summer or the chilly deeps of winter.

Iced Vodkaccino

1 ½ tbsp. chocolate cream liqueur, such as Baileys
1 ½ tbsp. heavy cream
1 ½ oz. vodka
3 oz. espresso or very strong brewed coffee,
cold or at room temperature

Combine liqueur and cream in a small bowl. Whisk until frothy and set aside. Pour vodka, then espresso, over cracked ice into a cocktail shaker. Shake vigorously, then strain into an old fashioned glass. Float frothed cream-liqueur mixture on top.

FOR YOUR FURTHER DRINKING PLEASURE: Don't be afraid to try other cream liqueurs with this drink. Vanilla adds a light and refreshing note, while nut flavors, such as almond and hazelnut, are perfect matches for coffee.

Hot Vodkaccino

1 ½ tbsp. chocolate cream liqueur, such as Baileys
1 ½ tbsp. heavy cream
4–6 oz. hot espresso or very strong brewed coffee
1 tsp. brown sugar
1 ½ oz. vodka

In a small saucepan over medium-low heat, heat liqueur and cream until warm, but do not allow to boil.

Pour the espresso into a mug. Add brown sugar and vodka and stir until sugar is dissolved. Whisk the hot liqueur-cream mixture until frothy and foamy and float on top of coffee mixture. Garnish with a dash of nutmeg or a sprinkle of cocoa powder.

FOR YOUR FURTHER DRINKING PLEASURE: If you're in the mood for something a bit easier, try **Russian Coffee**. Combine coffee, brown sugar, and vodka as directed above, then top with a dollop of chilled whipped cream. Another wintertime treat is the **Hot White Russian**, in which coffee liqueur replaces chocolate.

Vodkarita

We think it's a tragic accident that vodka wasn't around when the Margarita was invented. Fortunately, it's an error that can be easily remedied.

2 oz. vodka
1 oz. orange liqueur
1 oz. Rose's lime juice

Pour ingredients into a cocktail shaker filled with ice. Shake vigorously, then strain into a chilled cocktail glass and garnish with a lime wedge—and don't even think of rimming the glass with salt.

FOR YOUR FURTHER DRINKING PLEASURE: Almost all of your favorite Margarita variations will produce an equally excellent Vodkarita variation, starting with a **Frozen Vodkarita**, in which ingredients are combined in a blender with ice, whirred to a delightful slush, and poured into a chilled cocktail glass. There's also the delicious **Frozen Strawberry Vodkarita**, a Frozen Vodkarita in which 4 oz. thawed frozen strawberries in syrup are added to the blender, and a single large fresh strawberry is used as a garnish. And for sheer aesthetic value, we recommend a **Turquoise Vodkarita**, made like the original above with blue curaçao instead of plain orange liqueur and garnished with a slice of starfruit.

Windex

A drink with a name like this doesn't deserve to taste this good. Is there no justice?

1 ½ oz. vodka
½ oz. triple sec
½ oz. blue curaçao

Pour ingredients into a cocktail shaker filled with ice. Shake, then strain into a chilled cocktail glass.

Zaranes Cocktail

We have been completely unable to discover who Mr. Zaranes was—but we rather enjoy his cocktail.

1 ½ oz. vodka
1 ½ oz. apricot brandy
3 dashes Angostura bitters

Pour ingredients into a cocktail shaker filled with ice. Shake briskly, then strain into a chilled cocktail glass.

Infusions and Liqueurs

Vodka, that's an alcohol rub from the inside.

Bob Hope banters with Lucille Ball in *The Facts of Life*, 1960

It's no accident that the 1990s, the decade of new and exotic foods, gave rise to a passion for new and exotic vodkas, flavored to match the gourmet spirit of the times. Just one thing: The "new" trend wasn't really new at all. Russians and Poles had been flavoring their vodkas for centuries. Because early vodkas were crude, unreliable, and usually harsh, infusing became a way of smoothing and standardizing the product. Later, as methods of production advanced, and the end product became more refined, distillers vied with each other to create ever more distinctive and appealing varieties. Flavorings included a wide variety of fruits, spices, and herbs, including cherry, berries, lemon, pepper, dill, ginger, horseradish, and a variety of spicy roots and seeds.

WHY INFUSE?

Today, a wide variety of flavored vodkas are available, and if you're fond of vodka you probably already have a few of them in your liquor cabinet. So why, with all this plenitude, should you try making your own? Well,

"COCKTAILS"

the obvious reason is that you might come up with a variety that *isn't* available, or isn't available at a reasonable cost. And, since you can try infusions in mini-batches, you can avoid buying a large bottle of something you might not like all that well. But the real reason, and the best one, is that it's fun. There's something exciting about deciding what flavor you'd like, combining ingredients, waiting for the magic to happen, and sampling your efforts. And it's even more exciting when you come up with a hit, a unique vodka that tastes unlike anything you could buy at a store.

READY, SET, INFUSE

The first step in infusing vodka is assembling the equipment. There are a wide variety of special jars, almost all of them beautiful, some with spigots, some with impressive stands of wood or wrought iron. Our favorite site for tempting window-shopping of this sort is www.infused-vodka.com. You do not, however, need to invest any money at all to begin your career as a master infuser, as you probably have most of what you need scattered around your kitchen already.

TRADITIONAL INFUSED VODKAS

Kubanskaya: The forerunner of today's citrus vodkas, infused with dried lemon and orange peels.

Limonnaya: A barely sweetened lemon infusion, somewhere between lemon vodka and limoncello.

Okhotnichya: No Western equivalent quite matches this unique blend of coffee, lemon peel, spices, and fortified wine infusion, traditionally drunk by hunters to keep their strength up.

Pertsovka: Flavored with red chili peppers and black peppercorns, this infusion was one of the first to become a worldwide favorite.

Starka: Perhaps the oldest infusion, usually made with fortified wine and dried fruit.

Vishnyovka: Sour cherry infusion, still rare in America and Europe but common throughout Russia.

Zubrovka: A Polish vodka flavored with buffalo grass.

EQUIPMENT

The basic hardware needed to make infused vodkas at home is really very simple. The list includes:

✳ **GLASS JARS.** Almost any kind of jar will do, but it must be glass and have a tightly fitting lid. The lid can be metal, so long as it is coated—uncoated metal can interact with your infusion and affect the taste. Glass lids—such as the hinged ones with rubber seals that come on country-style storage jars, as well as cork stoppers, are also acceptable. The good news is that almost any clean, dry jar or bottle you happen to have will fit the bill—we've used pickle jars, empty liquor bottles, spaghetti sauce jars, well-scrubbed sauce bottles and jam jars, and a variety of other containers from our pantry. When choosing a jar, consider the volume of vodka you are going to infuse. Since the vodka needs to cover whatever you are infusing, using a large jar to infuse a little vodka will not produce the best results. Our favorite choice for small batches are maraschino cherry jars, which are about the right size and have a small mouth that makes pouring easier.

✳ **STRAINERS.** Most infusions should be strained, and we strain all of ours as a matter of course. There are two reasons for this. The first is aesthetic. Part of the mystique of vodka is its beautiful clarity, and you won't want any stray bits of seed or fruit spoiling the view. The exception to this is when you are leaving a particular ingredient—such as lemon peel or a sprig of rosemary—in the bottle on purpose. Even in this case, some items—such as berries—become unattractive after giving their best to the vodka, and should be replaced by a fresh, more attractive token representative. You will probably not need to go out and buy a strainer. An ordinary household strainer of fine wire mesh will do. Many people also have a golden fine mesh filter that came with a coffee machine and has never been used. If you can locate yours, it works like a charm. Paper coffee filters can be used in a pinch but we don't recommend them—they absorb a lot of the

vodka, are slow, and become soggy and need to be replaced if you are filtering a large amount of vodka.

✳ **FUNNELS.** If you are decanting your finished infusion into a small-mouthed bottle, such as the bottle the vodka originally came in, you will need a funnel to keep from spilling any of your precious creation.

✳ **LABELS.** You only *think* you'll remember what you infused with what and when. We strongly recommend putting a peel-and-stick label on every jar, making note of the ingredients, the amounts, and the start date as well as any special methods you tried, such as "crushed dill lightly" or "used frozen and thawed berries."

✳**NOTEBOOK OR NOTECARDS.** In addition to the kind of data above, you also want to keep track of the outcome of your experiments. How long did it take the infusion to reach its prime? Did you have to add or adjust ingredients along the way?

Would you take a different approach next time? A well-kept notebook of recipes and methods can, over time, become worth its weight in gold. Look what it did for the Smirnoff family when they fled the Russian Revolution and landed in Paris.

GUIDELINES

The first thing to understand about creating infusions is that it isn't a science. Because you're dealing with fresh ingredients, the results can vary depending on when and where they were grown, what the weather was like during the growing season, how the produce was handled, how long it took to reach the market, and a variety of other factors. That said, there are a few things to keep in mind as you begin:

✳ **INFUSE IN A GLASS.** As we mentioned above, make your infusions in glass bottles or jars that have tightly fitting lids. Metal and plastic should be avoided.

✳ **USE DECENT VODKA.** It's surprising how many people think that, since they're adding flavor to a "flavorless" spirit, any old vodka will do. This isn't true. A cheap vodka with a harsh finish will just become a cheap flavored vodka with a harsh finish. You don't need to spend a lot of money on a premium vodka, but the one you choose should be palatable on its own.

✳ **USE THE *RIGHT* VODKA.** There are some fine potato and rye vodkas out there, but most of the time they are the wrong choice for making an infusion. Because they have strong characteristics of their own, they can interfere with what you're trying to achieve.

✳ **USE PRODUCE IN SEASON IF POSSIBLE.** If you're working with fresh fruits, vegetables, or herbs, try to do your infusing in season if possible. Produce that has ripened naturally in the sun and has been picked at the peak of its growing cycle will have more color and flavor than off-season produce. If you crave peach vodka out of season, you will probably have better luck with ripe, good-quality peaches that have been frozen (without syrup or additives) than with pale, hard, flavorless peaches from a hothouse. Of course, this guideline doesn't apply if you're using dried fruits, sun-dried tomatoes, and dried spices such as vanilla beans.

✳ **WASH AND DRY FRESH PRODUCE THOROUGHLY.** We recommend washing all fruits, vegetables, and herbs before using, even if you plan to peel them. Once washed, allow them to dry completely before using.

✳ **LOOK FOR FROZEN PRODUCTS WITHOUT ADDITIVES.** There's nothing wrong with using frozen fruits in your infusions, whether from your own freezer or the grocer's. We do recommend, however, choosing products that have been packaged without sugar, syrups, or other additives, all of which can affect your infusion.

✳ **CUTTING FRUIT INTO SMALLER PIECES WILL SPEED THE INFUSION PROCESS.** This is especially helpful with large, dense fruits such as mango and pineapple.

✳ **PIERCE LARGE PIECES OF FRUIT WITH A FORK.** Many infusers like the look of large pieces of fruit for aesthetic reasons. And some fruits, such as apricots, will become pulpy if cut into pieces that are too small. For this reason, many infusers prefer to leave smaller fruits whole and larger fruits in halves, and pierce them in several places with the tines of a fork to facilitate the release of flavorful juices.

✳ **DECIDE WHICH ITEMS SHOULD BE PEELED.** Some fruits have skin that is not flavorful and will only impede the infusing process. This includes peaches, apricots, nectarines, mangoes, and the like, all of which should be peeled. On the other hand, citrus fruits have skins so rich in flavorsome oils that the peels alone can be used, provided they have had the bitter white pith scraped off and discarded. And some ingredients, such as tomatoes and plums, need their skins intact to keep the delicate inner flesh from disintegrating too quickly.

✳ GETTING BERRIES AND OTHER FRUITS TO "JUICE" SPEEDS THE INFUSION PROCESS. Berries and some other fruits, such as peaches, can be reluctant to yield their juices. There are two ways to give this process a head start. The first is to sprinkle the berries or fruit with a small amount of sugar, stir to distribute evenly, and let stand at room temperature. If you want to avoid using sugar, simply freeze and defrost the fruit—the freezing process will break down the juice-retaining tissues.

✳ SEEDS SHOULD BE LIGHTLY CRUSH-ED. If you're making an infusion with dried seeds—such as peppercorns, star anise, or caraway—remember that most seed casings are tough. Crushing the seeds lightly to crack the cases will facilitate the flavoring process. A good method is to place seeds in a freezer-weight plastic bag, wrap the bag in a tea towel, and tap it firmly with a rubber mallet or hammer.

✳ IF USING DRIED SPICES, USE WHOLE OR DRIED LEAF VARIETIES IF POSSIBLE.

You probably have the makings of an interesting vodka in your spice cupboard right now. Just remember to avoid the ground, powdered jars in favor of whole spices—like cloves and nutmeg—or dried, crumbled leaves—like oregano and tarragon. In general, use 1 rounded tablespoon dried spice to infuse 1 (750ml) bottle of vodka. If you do use ground spices, you will need to strain your finished infusion through cheesecloth or extremely fine mesh.

✳ FOR MOST INFUSIONS, ADD THE FLAVORING INGREDIENTS TO THE JAR FIRST, THEN THE VODKA. This is most important with fruit infusions. Letting the vodka wash gently over the ingredients as you fill the bottle will help the mingling begin.

✳ DON'T FILL TO THE BRIM. Many infusion ingredients—especially fruits and some vegetables—release juices during the infusion process, and you will end up with a bit more liquid than you began with. Because of this, it's important to leave some headroom in your infusion jar. If you're infusing in a vodka bottle, pour off a little of the vodka and enjoy a cocktail as you prepare the infusion.

✳ GIVE YOUR INFUSION A GOOD START. Once all the ingredients are in and the lid is secured, give your infusion bottle a good shake to get the flavoring process started. As the infusing process continues, regularly shake or stir to distribute flavors.

✳ KEEP INFUSIONS AWAY FROM THE LIGHT. Unless instructed otherwise, let your infusions work in the dark. You can do this by covering the jar with a towel, placing it in a cupboard, or finding a gloomy, out-of-the-way corner for it.

✳ INFUSE AT ROOM TEMPERATURE. There seems to be an ongoing debate about whether infusion should be done at room temperature or in the refrigerator. One advantage of cold infusing is that you will be able to taste the vodka at the proper chilled temperature as you go along. However, cold slows down the process, and it will take

longer for the flavor to develop. Therefore, we recommend infusing at room temperature and transferring the jar to the refrigerator as the infusion nears completion.

I don't think I can stand any more.

varga

✳ TASTE FREQUENTLY. As we said before, infusing is far from an exact science. Be prepared to taste your infusion daily so you'll know when to stop the process. Aside from helping you identify a good end product, frequent tasting will develop your palate and teach you a lot about how flavor develops and blooms.

✳ **WHEN YOU REACH THE PERFECT TASTE LEVEL, YOU MAY WANT TO STOP THE INFUSION.** You can do this by removing the flavoring ingredient. Sometimes, however, we enjoy leaving certain ingredients—such as the peel in lemon vodka—in the bottle a bit longer, and tingling our taste buds with the steadily intensifying flavors. All flavorings should be removed if they begin to look bleached, brown, or cloudy.

✳ **DON'T EXPOSE FLAVORING INGREDIENTS TO AIR.** If you choose to leave ingredients in while you drink the infusion, you will need to add more vodka from time to time. Flavoring ingredients should not be exposed to air, even the air inside a sealed bottle.

✳ **DECANT.** Finished infusions should be strained into clean, dry glass bottles or jars with tightly fitting lids.

✳ **STORE PROPERLY.** Infused vodkas should be stored upright, out of the light, at cool room temperature or in the refrigerator.

HOW LONG?

This, of course, is the big question. Once your infusion is jarred and working, how long will it be until you can enjoy the fruit of your labor? There is no clear answer to this question, and even experts with years of experience dispute the issue. One insists that strongly flavored fruits, like pineapple, require no more than a day or two, while an equally experienced infuser insists that because pineapple is dense and fibrous, it will take up to two weeks. And, while most infusions take from one day to two weeks, a few professionals let their infusions work for weeks to develop deep, strong flavors.

We can vouch for the unpredictability of the process and the virtues of patience, as the blueberry infusion we were told should take only three days was undrinkable until a week had passed. At the two-week mark it became so interesting we transferred it to the refrigerator, where, after a month, the stuff became so downright delicious we discarded the berries and considered it officially finished.

Why the wide disagreement on times? Do the so-called experts not know what they're talking about? Is our blueberry experience the definitive timetable for all blueberry infusions? Not necessarily. The only true guide is individual experience. As we said earlier, infusions can vary a good deal for a variety of reasons—from the freshness and ripeness of the ingredients, to the area and climate in which they were grown, to the way they were ripened, handled, and prepared, to the equipment used, the climate, and the conditions that prevailed during infusion.

There's also the matter of individual taste. What seems finished to one person's palate may seem pale and barely begun to another. Personal preference plays an enormous role here, as some people prefer infusions to have a mere hint of the flavor in question while others demand an almost liqueur-like intensity.

Given these wide variables, it's a better idea to taste your infusion daily, keep careful notes, and act as your own judge rather than follow arbitrary guidelines that may not give you the infusion you're looking for.

RECIPES FOR INFUSED VODKAS

If you skipped reading the guidelines for infusing, above, go back and do so now. Also, please note that all of these recipes are scaled for 1 (750ml) bottle of vodka. Feel free to test recipes in smaller quantities if you wish. Simply reduce the amounts proportionately. Here's the vital equation to remember: 750ml = 25 oz. = 3 c. plus 1 tbsp.

Other helpful measurement conversions can be found on pages 26–27.

Anise: According to biographers, anise-flavored vodka was a personal favorite of Peter the Great. Who's to quibble with a tsar? Not us, certainly. In the infusion jar, combine 30 pieces of star anise, cracked, and ¼ cup sugar. Add vodka and stir or shake to dissolve sugar. Shake again every few days.

Anise Seed: For a less sweet, slightly subtler infusion than the one above, place 1 rounded tsp. lightly crushed anise seeds in an infusion jar and add vodka.

Aquavit: Strictly speaking, aquavit is a spirit in its own right rather than an infused vodka. But since it can be a bit hard to find in some areas, we offer this recipe, which makes a fair facsimile. To your infusion jar add the following seeds, all lightly crushed: 1½ tsp. each of caraway, dill, and cumin, ¾ tsp. fennel, and 1 tsp. coriander. Next add 1 piece star anise, cracked, 1 whole clove, and a long strip of lemon or orange, scraped free of pith. Store in a cool, dark place for 2 weeks, shaking every 3 days. After 2 weeks, begin tasting and taste every 3 to 4 days until the desired strength is reached, then strain into a clean bottle and store in the freezer, along with shot glasses to drink it from.

Berry (mixed): In a bowl, combine ¼ cup each of raspberries, strawberries, blackberries, blueberries, cranberries that have been frozen and thawed, and cherries that have been pitted and halved. Toss with 2 tbsp. sugar to coat and transfer to infusion jar. Add vodka and shake or stir every few days to keep sugar from crystallizing.

Blueberry: In infusion jar, place 1 pint whole blueberries that have been frozen and thawed, along with any juices that result from the thawing. Add 1 oz. raspberry liqueur, then pour in vodka.

Buffalo Grass: Buffalo grass grows wild all over America's Great Plains, but before you pick yourself a bunch of trouble, make absolutely sure that what you have is indeed buffalo grass and that it has never been treated with pesticide, herbicides, or other chemicals. Once you've cleared that bar, place a dozen blades in your infusion jar and add vodka.

Caraway: Place 1 rounded tbsp. caraway seeds, lightly crushed, in a clean infusion jar and add vodka. Let steep in a cool, dark place, shaking from time to time.

Cherry: Pit and halve 4 pints (8 cups)

Bing cherries, place in a large infusion jar, and pour in vodka. If you want a hint of sweetness, add ½ vanilla bean, slit open, or 2 to 3 tsp. almond extract. The large amount of cherries makes for quick infusion and vodka-macerated fruit that is firm and delicious. Save the cherries after you strain the vodka and enjoy them with ice cream or sorbet.

Chili: There are endless recipes for chili vodka, and most of them are quite good. Which you prefer is essentially a matter of how fiery you like your spirits, and which peppers you prefer. To get started, we recommend using 1 cup fresh chili peppers. Which varieties are up to you, and some people prefer a single-note infusion made with just one variety, such as jalapeño or habanero. We prefer the complexity of a mix that includes both hot and mild, red and green, but encourage you to use whatever most appeals to you. The peppers should be slit or, if they are very large, cut into chunks. Scraping out the seeds will result in a milder infusion, and we recommend leaving at least some of the seeds intact, lest your infusion be too weak. Place the chilies in an infusion jar and add vodka.

Cinnamon: To infusion jar, add a total of 12 inches of cinnamon sticks, broken into 2- to 4-inch lengths. Add vodka.

Cinnamon Apple: Follow the recipe above but add 1 Granny Smith apple, 1 Golden Delicious apple, and 1 crisp red apple, each cored and cut into sixths.

Citrus: Cut 1 lemon, 1 orange or blood orange, and 1 small ruby grapefruit into pieces, leaving the rinds on. Place in infusion jar and add vodka. Note that you can vary the flavor by slightly altering your fruit mix, exchanging the orange for tangerine, for example, or the lemon for lime.

Coriander: Place 1 rounded tbsp. cracked coriander seeds in an infusion jar and add vodka.

Cranberry: Place 1 cup frozen and thawed cranberries in an infusion jar and add 8 whole cloves, 1 whole cracked nutmeg, 1 (3-inch) cinnamon stick, and ½ vanilla bean, slit open. Pour in vodka.

Cucumber: Peel ½ seedless (English)

cucumber and cut into long spears. Place in infusion jar. Add the zest of 1 small lemon, then pour in vodka.

Currant: Place 1 cup fresh black currants in infusion jar. Add 2 sugar cubes and pour in vodka.

Dill: It's best to make this vodka in a narrow bottle rather than a wide jar—it keeps the dill from floating on the surface and ensures maximum infusion. Cram as much fresh dill as you can into the empty bottle. When the bottle is half full, add a lump of sugar, then continue packing in dill. When the bottle is full, add vodka.

Garlic and Dill: Flatten or crush 1 giant or 1½ regular-sized cloves garlic and place in infusion jar. Add 3 sprigs fresh dill, then vodka. If you desire a bit more bite, add 4 white peppercorns, cracked.

Gazpacho: This vodka is excellent on its own or in a spicy Bloody Mary. To the infusion jar, add 8 cherry tomatoes, 1 tsp. celery seed, a few sprigs of parsley, 1 small onion, cut into quarters, 12 pieces pickled okra or pickled green beans or a blend of both, 1 Anaheim chili, split lengthwise,

and 1 serrano chili, split lengthwise. Shake or stir to distribute ingredients, then add vodka.

Ginger: Place 12 oz. crystallized ginger in infusion jar and add vodka. Or peel 1 or 2 hands fresh ginger, place in infusion jar, and cover with vodka. Ginger hands may be broken into large pieces if you wish. This vodka infuses very quickly, so be careful not to let it get too strong.

Grapefruit: Leaving the peel on, cut 1 ruby grapefruit into chunks and add vodka.

Herbs: Try infusions with a variety of fresh herbs, such as rosemary, tarragon, basil, thyme, cilantro, lemongrass, mint, and sage.

Horseradish: In infusion jar, put 2 oz. fresh horseradish, peeled and chopped. Add 1 tbsp. celery seed, lightly crushed, and 2 tbsp. black peppercorns, cracked. If you want a bit more kick, add a small dried red chili pepper. Pour in vodka and begin tasting the next day.

Lemon: Depending on how lemony you like your vodka, and how quickly you want it to infuse, use 1 to 2 lemons for this. With a zester or vegetable peeler, peel in long thin ribbons, taking only the yellow part. Scrape away any white pith, then place in infusion jar and add vodka.

Lemon Pepper: Following the method above, use the peel of 1 lemon and add 1 tbsp. black peppercorns, cracked. Mix in infusing jar and add vodka.

Lemon Thai Pepper: Follow the recipe for lemon pepper vodka, above, and add 2 fresh Thai chilies, slit open (jalapeños may be substituted). Mix in infusing jar and add vodka.

Lime: Cut 1 lime into quarters and add vodka. It's extremely important to remove the fruit when the vodka reaches its peak, as lime left in too long becomes bitter and will spoil your infusion.

Melon: Combine 2 cups each of cantaloupe and honeydew melon, rinds and seeds removed, in infusing jar and add vodka.

Olive: Drain 1 6-oz. jar green olives that have been pitted but not stuffed. Save the brine for Dirty Martinis (page 83), place the olives in infusion jar, and add vodka. After the infusion is finished, use the olives as garnish or serve as snacks.

Orange: Follow the method for lemon or lime vodkas, above.

Peach: Dip 6 large or 10 smaller ripe peaches in boiling water for 4 seconds, then remove. Peel and cut in quarters, discarding skin and stones. Place in infusion jar and add vodka.

Pear: Cut 1 Bosc pear, 1 Comice pear, and 1 Bartlett pear into quarters. Leave skin on but cut out and discard core. Place in infusion jar and add vodka. If you want to spice your infusion, consider adding one of the following: 1 small cinnamon stick, 1 cracked nutmeg, several whole cloves, or 1 piece crystallized ginger.

Pepper, Chili: See Chili, page 127.

Peppercorn: Place 2 to 3 tbsp. cracked black peppercorns in an infusion jar and

add vodka. The more peppercorns you use, the faster this vodka will infuse—but be prepared to strain and decant your vodka after as little as a day, as the peppercorns will go right on flavoring the vodka.

Pineapple: Our first try at this was somewhat disappointing—possibly because we live in the North, and tend to get pineapples that were harvested a bit green. However, we overcame this by bruising the cut-up pineapple pieces with the pestle from our mortar and pestle set. Clean, trim, core, and cut pineapple into wedges to make 2 cups. Bruise (but don't mash) the pieces with a mortar or similar blunt, heavy utensil. Transfer to infusion jar and add vodka.

Raspberry: Place 2 pints (4 cups) raspberries in an infusion jar and cover with vodka.

Saffron: The flavor of saffron is delicate and interesting, but it's the color of this one that's a show stopper. To your infusion jar, add ½ teaspoon saffron threads. Add vodka gently, pouring against the side of the jar, to avoid pulverizing the saffron.

Strawberry: Clean and halve 4 pints (8

cups) strawberries. Place in an infusion jar and cover with vodka.

Tea: Add 2 tbsp. leaves of your favorite strong tea to infusion jar and pour in vodka. Traditional Russians would use black tea, but a more modern, Asian fusion choice would be green. In either case, tea with added fruit notes—such as peach or berry—can also produce a flavorful infusion.

Tomato: Place 12 large pieces sun-dried tomato (dry, not oil-packed) in infusion jar and add vodka.

Tomato *Arrabiata*: To produce a vodka with the spicy bite of arrabiata sauce, follow the recipe above, add 1 clove garlic, smashed and peeled, and 1 tsp. hot red pepper flakes. If your pepper flakes are fresh and potent, 1 tsp. will do. If your flakes are older, more may be needed. Our advice is to start with the smaller amount and add more if needed.

Tomato *Pomodoro*: If you'd like an infusion with subtle Italian flavor, follow the recipe for tomato vodka, above, and add 2 long sprigs each of fresh basil and oregano, or 2 tsp. each of dried crumbled basil and oregano.

Vanilla: Slit 1 vanilla bean lengthwise and lay open. Scrape out the seeds and place them in infusion jar. Cut the bean in half and add it too, then add vodka.

Watermelon: Put 2 cups seeded watermelon cubes in infusion jar, along with any juice released when cutting up the watermelon, then add vodka. If your watermelon is ripe and juicy, this infusion may mature in less than a day. It is particularly delicious sipped ice cold, straight from the freezer.

RESCUING A FAILED INFUSION

It happens to all great inventors from time to time—something just didn't work out as planned. If you're going to experiment with infusions, every once in a while you will create something that just isn't pleasing to your palate. Before you pour it down the drain, consider one of these options.

✳ **TASTE COLD.** Infusions are best sampled cold, and sampling at room temperature will not give you a true reading. Please see our guidelines for tasting vodkas on page 16.

✳ HAVE PATIENCE. We can't tell you how many lackluster infusions improved when we gave them more time—often much more time than guidelines and common sense suggested. An unfinished flavor will have something of a split personality—you will taste the flavoring, and you will taste the vodka. Because the flavor can be detected, many amateur infusers conclude they have an infusion, just not a very good one. However, a truly finished infusion will not have this split personality. It will not be two competing identities but a completely melded blend.

✳ STRENGTHEN. If the flavor is too weak, adding more flavoring ingredients may help. Depending on the type of infusion, you may also consider adding a flavor booster, such as a touch of sugar or a bit of vanilla

✳ DILUTE. An infusion that is too strong can be redeemed by diluting it with more vodka. To do this, strain and discard the flavoring ingredients, then add vodka gradually until you achieve the right level of taste. Reseal and store.

✳ CREATE A LIQUEUR. Less than spectacular fruit or spiced infusions can often be transformed into palatable liqueurs. To see if your ugly duckling can become a swan, measure out a small amount of vodka and add some simple syrup. If you come up with something you like, sweeten the entire batch.

✳ CONSIDER COOKING. If your infusion is simply disappointing rather than truly distasteful, consider cooking with it. A tomato vodka that isn't quite pleasing on its own might be fine for vodka penne, for example.

✳ USE IT ANYWAY. A pale infusion that lacks distinctiveness on its own can be used in a variety of compatible cocktails. As long as you don't expect it to contribute a strong flavor note, you'll be fine.

SWEET INFUSIONS

In addition to infused vodkas, there are infusions that are substantially sweetened, and more closely akin to liqueurs or contemporary schnapps (traditional schnapps were not as sweet as today's products). The Russians called these products *navlikas*, but even in this category the degree of sweetness could vary considerably. There are fine lines between an infused vodka in which a small amount of sugar is an ingredient, a lightly sweetened *navlika*, and a true liqueur.

There's also a fine line between when a sweetened concoction ceases being a vodka product and becomes something in its own right. Because vodka has minimal flavor, it is the perfect spirit base for all sorts of intensely flavored liqueurs. Our advice is to not fuss too much over nomenclature, but find something you like and enjoy it!

To keep your experimentation budget in bounds, we have scaled these recipes to make relatively small batches. To increase the amount of finished product, simply multiply the recipe accordingly.

Amaretto

½ c. sugar
¼ c. brown sugar
1 c. vodka
1 tbsp. almond extract
1 tsp. vanilla extract

Combine sugars and ½ cup water to make simple syrup (see page 35). When syrup has cooled, stir in vodka and extracts, transfer to a sealed bottle, and store out of the light. Because extracts are used to flavor this liqueur it will be ready to drink within a day.

Anisette

½ c. sugar
1 c. vodka
10 pieces star anise

Combine sugar and ½ cup water to make simple syrup (see page 35). When syrup has cooled, stir in vodka and anise and store in a cool, dark place for 2 to 4 weeks.

Apricot

⅔ c. sugar
6 oz. peeled, pitted fresh apricots
1 c. vodka

Combine sugar and ⅔ cup water in a heavy saucepan and bring to a boil, stirring to dissolve sugar. Reduce heat, add apricots, and simmer gently for about 5 minutes. Remove apricots and set aside. When syrup has cooled to room temperature, add vodka and test for viscosity. If the liqueur is too thick, thin with a little water. Now test for taste. If your apricots were picked at the peak of ripeness, the liqueur may be fully flavored and the apricots can be discarded. If you would like a stronger flavor, return the apricots to the liqueur. A bit of lemon or orange zest can also be added. Pour into a bottle, seal, and let infuse for about 1 month, then strain into a clean bottle.

Blackberry

1 c. fresh blackberries
½ c. sugar
1 c. vodka

Place blackberries in a bottle. Add sugar and shake to coat. Add vodka, seal, and gently shake again. Let infuse in a cool, dark place for 6 to 8 weeks, shaking once a week. Strain finished liqueur into a clean bottle.

Blueberry

1 c. vodka
½ c. sugar
1 ½ c. fresh blueberries, washed and picked over

Combine vodka and sugar in jar and stir to dissolve sugar. Add blueberries, shake gently, and seal jar. Store in a cool, dark place for 6 to 8 weeks, gently shaking every other week. Strain finished liqueur into a clean bottle.

Coffee

1 ⅓ c. brown sugar, lightly packed
3 level tbsp. instant coffee
1 c. vodka
Dash of vanilla extract

Combine sugar, coffee, and 1 cup water in a heavy saucepan. Bring to a boil, reduce the heat, and simmer for 15 minutes, stirring occasionally. Remove from the heat and let cool to room temperature. Stir in vodka and vanilla. Transfer to a bottle and store in a cool, dark place.

Cytrynivka

(SPICED LEMON)
2 lemons
1 tbsp. coriander seeds, lightly crushed
2 whole cloves
1 c. vodka
1 c. sugar

Cut lemons into quarters or slices, leaving peel on, and place in jar. Add coriander and cloves, pour in vodka, and infuse at room temperature for 1 week.

Combine sugar and 1 cup water to make simple syrup (see page 35). Cool and set aside. Strain the vodka lemon mixture into the cooled syrup and stir well. If necessary, strain a second time. Transfer to a bottle, seal, and let infuse in a cool, dark place for 2 more weeks.

Limoncello

5 Meyer lemons
½ c. sugar
1 c. vodka

Using a zester or vegetable peeler, remove the peel from the lemons in long, thin strips, taking only the yellow part. Scrape off any of the white pith that remains, and place the zest in a small bottle. (You can save the lemons to make pie or lemonade.) Add sugar and shake to distribute, then pour in vodka. Seal bottle tightly and shake vigorously. Shake daily for 2 weeks, then taste. Strain finished Limoncello into a clean bottle.

Limoncello Lime

Follow the method above using the peels from 2 to 3 limes instead of lemons and increasing the amount of sugar to ¾ cup.

Medivka

(HONEY)
Zest of ½ orange or lemon
1 whole clove
¼ to ½ tsp. allspice
Pinch of nutmeg
⅓ c. dark honey, such as buckwheat

Place zest and spices in a small saucepan. Cover with 6 tbsp. water and simmer over low heat for 15 minutes. Do not boil. Place honey in a second saucepan and strain spiced liquid into it. Stir to combine, then bring to a simmer. Skim off any foam that comes to the surface. Over low heat, gently warm vodka in a third saucepan and add the honey mixture, stirring to thoroughly combine. Allow to cool, then pour into a clean bottle and seal.

Peppermint

2 tbsp. plus 2 tsp. sugar
1 c. light corn syrup
1 c. vodka
1 tsp. peppermint extract

Combine sugar and corn syrup in a heavy saucepan. Warm over medium heat until sugar dissolves, stirring constantly, about 5 minutes. Remove from the heat and stir in vodka. Cover the saucepan and set aside until cooled to room temperature. Stir in peppermint extract and transfer to a clean bottle for storage.

Pineapple

8 oz. fresh pineapple chunks
½ c. sugar
1 c. vodka

Place pineapple chunks in a clean jar. Combine sugar and ½ cup water to make simple syrup (see page 35). When syrup has cooled, stir in vodka and pour over pineapple. Seal, shake, and store in a cool, dark place. Taste after 2 to 4 weeks. When fully flavored, strain into a clean bottle and seal.

Spice

½ c. vodka

1 c. sugar

1 ½ tsp. ground cloves

½ tsp. ground cinnamon

½ tsp. ground nutmeg

½ tsp. ground allspice

⅛ tsp. vanilla extract

Combine vodka, sugar, and ½ cup water in a heavy saucepan and warm over low heat, stirring until sugar is dissolved. Remove from the heat and stir in spices and vanilla. Transfer to a clean bottle or jar, cap, and let stand in a cool, dark place for about 2 weeks, then taste. When the liqueur is finished, strain through several layers of cheesecloth or an extremely fine mesh to remove spices. Pour into clean bottle and seal.

Vishnyovka

(SOUR CHERRY)
1 c. pitted and halved sour cherries
½ c. sugar
1 c. vodka

Place cherries in a jar and add sugar. Cover the jar and shake until cherries are coated with sugar. Pour in vodka and shake a few more times. Store in a cool, dark place for 4 weeks, then strain into a bottle and seal.

VARIATION: Some people like their Vishnyovka spiced—try adding a 1-inch cinnamon stick or ½ tsp. ground cinnamon and a pinch of ground nutmeg. (If using ground spices, strain the finished product through several layers of cheesecloth). Store in a clean bottle.

THROW A PARTY!

So many infusions, so little time. A great way to taste them all is to hold an **Infusion Party**. Give your guests a few weeks' notice, and tell each one he or she will be responsible for bringing at least one bottle of a homemade vodka infusion. Coordinate who will bring what to ensure a broad selection, and be prepared to offer guidance and tips for novice infusers. We got enthusiastic cooperation when we attached a different infusion recipe to each invitation we sent. On the night of the party, you'll be rewarded with a stunning selection of vodkas to try. (For pointers on how to taste vodka, please see page 16.)

INDEX

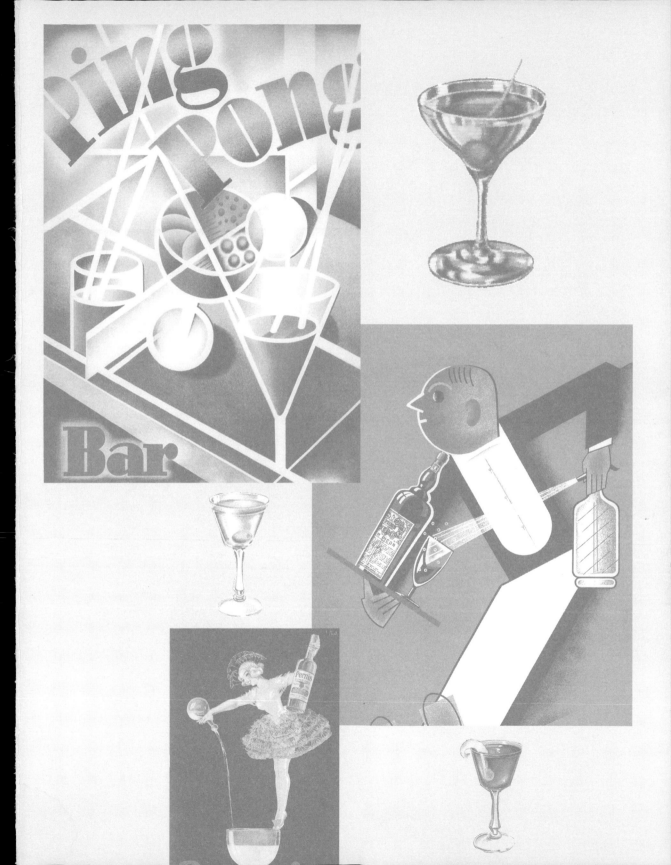